To call this book a great value  want to dramatically increase in the coming weeks and mo... and overall workload, read this immediately. If I were to g... real estate, Alina is the first person I'd call. When it comes to dominating a market, she's the best in the world.

Frank Kern, President, FrankKern.com

Alina Schumacher is not just a real estate expert, she has the incredible ability to help people balance life with career success and achieve the best of both. Think of yourself as 'Real' estate, who you are and what you want, then follow the secrets in the book to finally achieve your financial and personal goals. I'm proud to call Alina my friend.

Roger Love, Celebrity Voice Coach & Top-Selling Author, Hollywood

I have been in the real estate business for over 35 years and Alina Schumacher brings a cutting-edge distinction to the industry. The market is a highly competitive one, that has undergone so much change, that it is almost the fabric of our daily life. Each skill brings the power of truth and incorporates self-talk to bring about world-class agent application. This book is a must for any real estate agent or company because it lays out the foundation for growth and success. I consider this book to be the "Real Estate Bible" for highly successful real estate agents.

Kim Erwin, REALTOR®, Keller Williams Island Properties, TX

Alina's book is intelligent, insightful, creative and compassionate in terms of building your business and making your work MATTER in your life! Hers is not a "get rich quick" scheme or a self centered pack of mantras to get to your first million. No, this is an invitation to invest in matters of the heart. Both yours as a real estate agent and the hearts of the lives you get to touch along the way. There's plenty of practical hard working advice that works! My business and my heart have been transformed.

Linda Christensen, REALTOR®, Keller Williams Realty, Nevada

Dominating your market begins with Alina Schumacher. She's dominated as a Realtor, Agency Owner and is showing herself to be a dominant Coach and Teacher in Real Estate. Her empathy and insights in this book are leading agents in this fast paced, focused, digital age.

Vince Green, Marketing Coach, Clickfunnels

Once I started reading this book, I could not put it down. Her story from struggle to success resonated with me and inspired me. Her framework for Real Estate Professionals is tangible – something all of us can go after. My entire team will be reading this book and I advise the same for others.

Nate Armstrong, President of Home Invest, Sarasota, FL

Alina takes you through an insightful journey to find the tips to make you a world-class agent and live in your true greatness. These 10 skills really are indispensable if you want to take your business to 300+ sides. You've gotta live them and you've gotta own them! Alina will deliver insight and bring your thinking to a different level.

Kerby Skurat, Team Leader of the #40 RE/MAX Team in Nation 2014

Alina did what very few people in our industry manage to do. With a very modest background, she skyrocketed to the top of our industry. These top 10 skills will give you the confidence to launch or grow your real estate business just like she did. She has a true servant's heart and you can tell when you read this book. She has fought the battles and did it the hard way so that you don't have to.

Lars Hedenborg, Ranked #14 in US for RE/MAX in 2014, RealEstateBSchool.com

I have read this book once and found it so intriguing I am rereading and studying it like a textbook when I was pursuing my doctorate! Get it, read it, soak in the insights.

Scott Oren, RE/MAX Professional Advantage, IL

Since I've been studying your work, I feel so much more confident. Not the kind ego crazy realtor jerk but more knowledgeable, poised, professional, and more qualified to do a great job for my seller clients. Thank you very much!

Kimberly Bagni, Four Seasons Realty Partners at LAER, Northborough, MA

It would be a very good use of your time to read this book! Alina is truly amazing and one of a kind. Her insight has been a huge win for me, personally!

Carl White, The Mortgage Marketing Animals, FL, USA

Alina's ability to set the stage and almost read my mind was incredible. She left me wanting more chapter after chapter and yet, always came through with answers to the questions I had. It is not one of those 'read and leave you hanging to sign up for the next program' type books. It will honestly change your life. It did mine.

Kelsey Findlay, Findlay RE Team, BC, Canada

HOW TO GET LISTINGS & DOMINATE YOUR MARKET

... Even If Nobody's Ever Heard Of You!

*Master The 10 Skills Of World-Class Agents
And Live The Life Of Your Dreams.*

ALINA SCHUMACHER

How To Get Listings and Dominate Your Market Even If Nobody's Ever Heard Of You.

Master The 10 Skills Of World-Class Agents
And Live The Life Of Your Dreams.

ISBN: 978-1-64746-034-1 Paperback

ISBN: 978-1-64746-035-8 Hardback

ISBN: 978-1-64746-036-5 Ebook

Library of Congress Number: 2019918657

DEDICATION

*To my husband, Andy, and our three children,
Kristina, Ben, and Marie.
I love you with all my heart, no matter what,
forever and always.*

And to my Mom who taught me to never give up.

INTRODUCTION AND ...
A WARNING (OF ALL THINGS)

I don't think I've ever read a book that started with a warning. You probably haven't either, and as you're about to find out, this is not a *traditional* kind of book. You didn't pay a traditional price for it, nor is the formatting and writing style anything like you'd expect in a *normal* book. I might break a few more rules ... let's see.

This is also not one of those get-rich-quick kind of books that over-promise and underdeliver. It's not about a sensational marketing strategy that may have at some point worked in one market and is totally unrealistic everywhere else. **It's not about a rags-to-riches kind of unicorn story** that is super inspiring but hard to apply to your own life and business. And finally, it's not just a teaser about the *what*—without actually giving you the *how*.

This book contains the blueprint that will help you to build a true real estate empire—regardless of where you are located and what level you're starting from. But it will only work if you do. As you commit to reading and studying the content and using it as your success guide, it is also my hope that **you will discover all of the secret gold nuggets I've hidden in-between the lines.** Each one of those gold nuggets has the potential to *10x your business* <u>on more levels</u> than you may currently realize. Keep re-reading the chapters at least once every quarter, and those 'directional signs' will appear when you're ready for them.

The principles, strategies, and tactics that I'll be sharing with you are exactly what I used to build my real estate business quickly and from scratch. As a matter of fact, I was a new immigrant to Canada and **barely spoke English** at that time. And even though this may sound totally crazy, in my second full year in real estate, I became the #1 local agent in my market area. Shortly after, I worked myself up to the top 1% of all REALTORS® in our province/board, and I've held that rank for many years and for as long as I've been selling real estate.

Over the years, I've seen so many agents enter this business, excited and passionate to serve people, but because they didn't really know where to start, they ended up making the same costly mistakes I made when I started out.

And honestly, even though I cannot spare you of *all* the growing pains, I can help you to significantly shorten your journey—and even more importantly—show you *how to do the right things in the right order*. If you're ready to play at that level, and finally succeed in real estate *and* in life, let's get started.

Actually, before we do … since you and I have probably never met, here's a quick and condensed version of my story, all the way from where I came from, why I decided to go into real estate, along with those painful, early day struggles of **not knowing *WHAT* to do, what to say, or *HOW* to say it, and as a result, losing opportunities, and being rejected over and over again.** Then, to eventually figuring out what *really* works in this business, and how to get it *without* having to sacrifice your health and your most important relationships in life.

If you'd rather get straight to the content, just jump to page 1.

If you'd like to understand my *Why* however, and what really drove me to seek the path to success and financial freedom, keep reading.

MY STORY

Having been born in communist Russia and having moved to Germany in my early teen years, I would have *never* dreamed that my journey would one day lead me to settle in Canada. And even though I could probably fill volumes with all the crazy stories, incredible experiences, and life lessons I've learned during those years; I'll leave that for another time.

Life was good. I was happily married to the man of my dreams, we had three beautiful babies, and we lived on a lovely acreage just outside of Cologne—picture perfect with a small vegetable garden, happy chickens, and about a dozen apple trees that provided us with hundreds of pounds of the most delicious apples every year. Best of all, we had the sweetest neighbors we could have ever asked for.

We had inherited this old little farmhouse from my husband's grandparents, and over the years, we had renovated and updated pretty much everything in that place. My husband didn't believe in debt or taking out loans, and so we did things slowly according to our budget. The result was charming—if you're into *Old English, Laura Ashley* style decor, that is.

The year we were finally finished, and there was no more construction, and no more dust, however, we had this crazy idea and ultimate dream of immigrating to Canada, inspired by some good friends, who were talking about this thing called homeschooling. It was a totally new concept for us. I mean, **who ever heard of such a thing?**

What parent could ever be qualified enough to teach their kids? It seemed strange and yet fascinating to us, and as with so many things in life, once you are brave enough to question the traditional methods and systems, **and start asking different questions,** you end up with entirely different answers.

There was just one problem…

Homeschooling was illegal, and in fact, prosecuted in Germany, and our new-found convictions were put to the test. Was *that* really worth the sacrifice of leaving everything, and more importantly, everyone dear to us behind?

Have you ever come to a fork in the road in your life where you knew that regardless of what path you'd take, nothing would ever be the same again?

It was one of those life-altering moments for us.

We had heard so much about Canada and the vast, untamed beauty of this country. But what appealed most to us was its multiculturalism. It seemed like the perfect place to raise our children, and we decided to go for it.

Having said that, I knew that this wouldn't be easy. It meant learning another new language, understanding a new culture, making a new home, new friends, new jobs, and embracing new opportunities that usually come with their share of change and challenges. It was a huge step out of our comfort zone, but we knew it was what we were meant to do.

And we were so glad we did, even though that first year was extra challenging. My husband was making twelve dollars an hour trying to support our family while studying for his electrician red seal challenge exams to get his license recognized here in Canada. And I remember our first year here … we couldn't even afford to buy a Christmas tree and Christmas presents for our kids.

And even though I had my hands full with a three, five, and seven-year-old, I was racking my brain trying to figure out what in the world I could do to supplement the family income from home, when someone suggested this agency that was looking for people who could **proofread Harley Davidson motorcycle repair manuals** that had been translated from English into German.

All right then … I jumped on it! They paid me ten dollars an hour, and I was able to do the projects from home whenever the kids were sleeping. And **every extra dollar helped!**

A few months in, though, it was killing me—more specifically, my neck and shoulders. Besides, I felt like I had so much more to offer to this world than looking for typos within oil change instructions … with all due respect to my Harley Davidson friends.

The opportunity to go into real estate presented itself just a few months later, and yet, **as lucrative as it sounded, it seemed totally impossible.**

I didn't know anybody. I didn't know the area. I had no business experience and no college education. I didn't have the slightest idea about local construction methods, and since English is my fourth language, you can probably imagine the language barrier I struggled with at that time. Besides, **this wasn't even why we came here!** I was looking for a side job, not a business.

I kept thinking about it though. Homeschooling was most certainly our priority—*but don't people usually look at houses in the evenings and on weekends?* Couldn't I be showing houses when my husband was home from work and able to watch the kids? Couldn't we make this work somehow?

I mean, **imagine if I made even just one single sale a month!** Or even every two months … that would change everything for us!

Long story short, after a lot of deliberation, my husband and I figured I should give it a shot, take the first exam, and if I managed to pass, we would take that as a sign to keep going. Well, that first exam came back at 94%, **even though I needed a dictionary** to make sure I understood all the words and the exam questions correctly.

But you know what they say—where there is a will there is way, and I was driven by a very strong desire to support my husband.

There may have been just a tiny little bit of selfishness in the mix, because after shoveling our 200' long driveway that entire first winter, I was determined that the following year we would be able to not only afford a Christmas tree **but also … a snowblower.**

There was also this quiet, unspoken dream inside my heart of being able to give our children a lifestyle I never had when I was growing up.

Don't get me wrong, they had everything they needed—most importantly, a loving and peaceful home. But I believe **there's more to life than just being able to pay the bills and go on vacation once a year.** I wanted our children not only to understand what it means to have, but how it feels to give.

Perhaps you can imagine what it might have been like growing up in Russia in the eighties, being of German descent. We didn't have much, and my German last name made me quite unpopular in school. I was labeled with words like "German pig" and "fascist." I guess it was *bullying* before bullying really was a thing.

My mom and I lived in **rooming apartments** since that was all we could afford at the time, where we shared dilapidated bathrooms and tiny kitchens that were **infested with rats,** with other co-tenants. Things constantly got stolen, and I will never forget the feeling of constant fear and unrest, because one of the co-tenants, an old bachelor, would often come home drunk. He would yell and throw up all over the bathroom, and my poor mother would have to clean the mess.

We all have a story.

We all have dreams and aspirations, and I believe that wanting more for your family is a beautiful thing. And I will be forever grateful to my parents for modelling that to me and being brave enough to migrate from Russia to Germany just as soon as the borders opened after so many years of people not being permitted to leave.

So where was I again … oh yes, my real estate license. It took me about six months to go through all the workbooks and write the three required exams, and I spent quite a few long nights studying pretty much until dawn, getting a couple of hours of sleep, and then going back to being a mom and homeschooling my children during the day.

I can't even tell you how happy I was when I finally had my license, and yet, it was really just the beginning. I had absolutely no idea what I had gotten myself into, and that was probably a good thing. I was very naive, like most aspiring new agents, talking about how much I *loved looking at homes* and *how I would just love showing people houses.*

Word eventually began to spread, and people referred to me as *"that German Immigrant girl that just started in real estate."* And what could she possibly have to offer at her age, lack of connections, and poor English skills?

I knew if I wanted to get anywhere with this new profession of mine, I would need to figure out how to find buyers and sellers. The terms "qualified buyer" and "motivated seller" entered the stage much later.

Meanwhile, *I was burning the candle at both ends,* wasting precious time and my very limited energy chasing people who didn't know what they wanted, arriving home late and completely drained and exhausted, to see my beautiful babies and my frazzled husband … along with piles of laundry and a sink full of dishes.

Somehow, this side job had turned into a *monster.* It was taking over my life, and I felt so desperately guilty, but I was still clinging on to hope. It seemed that the more I wanted it to work, though, the more dead-end roads I encountered.

I remember presenting my very first offer, feeling like a deer in headlights. I had no idea what to say and felt so inadequate.

There was so much to learn. More times than I could count, I remember having conversations with clients, **not understanding many of the words they were using, trying so hard to catch on to what they were saying and not letting them notice.**

When I finally got back home, I would try to look up those words in the dictionary *(if I could figure out their spelling)*, write them down in a notebook, memorize them, and try to incorporate them into my daily vocabulary. I still have a long way to go.

We're all on a journey, aren't we?

Eventually, and with a lot of trial and error, <u>and more mistakes and embarrassing bloopers than I'd want to admit</u> (the immigrant learning journey makes for an interesting life); in my second full year in real estate, I made it to the top 3% of all agents within our real estate board. Shortly after, <u>I worked myself up to the top 1%</u> of the 1600+ agents at that time, and … **we bought that snowblower.**

And you know, just when I thought I had it all figured out, I had this crazy idea of starting my own brokerage, which took my learning journey to a whole new level. <u>It was easier than teaching Calculus, though,</u> which is why my genius husband took over the homeschooling part, and all three of our students have since successfully graduated from high school ... while I missed my chance of finally getting educated.

Looking back, I can share with you that even though it is absolutely amazing to get to the point of true market domination—**where your signs are all over town,** and people <u>recognize and respect you</u>—your business runs like a really well-oiled machine because of the world-class support team and systems you've built, nothing could adequately describe the overwhelming feeling of gratitude I have in my heart, because by the grace of God and a lot of hard work, we were not only able to create an amazing lifestyle for our family and travel to all kinds of places, but we were also able to teach our kids about entrepreneurship, persistence, compassion, and the incredible joy of sharing what we have with the less fortunate in this world. And that just lights me up!

Has it been easy?

Definitely not. Nothing in life worth having ever comes easy. *And although I did many things right, I did so many more things wrong,* making a painful amount of <u>unnecessary and totally avoidable</u> mistakes that, sadly, came with a huge price tag. I suppose that is what they call it the school of **hard knocks.** I know it so well I bet I'd make a pretty decent tour guide.

Had I only known then what I know now.

Over the years so many people have asked me how I was able to do it all, given my circumstances, while the average agent in North America struggles to sell an average of five homes per year, and the answer to that question has become my life's work.

To become a competitive player in the market on that level requires a very different way of thinking, preparation, and execution. And if you are ready to play at that level and build a true real estate empire—without the overwhelm, the detours, and the burnout—buckle your seatbelt and let's go!

THE DINNER EXPERIENCE

One of my favorite places in the world to dine at is at the Gustino restaurant, located at the JW Marriott Resort & Spa in Cancun, Mexico.

From the moment you enter the foyer of that restaurant, you have this unmistakable feeling that you're about to experience something very special. There's just something about it!

As you make your way down the winding staircase, you walk through a wide hallway that gives you a generous peek into the kitchen area and all the delightful things that are being made there from scratch.

And I wish I could even remotely describe the intoxicating smell of all the freshly baked breads, the rich basil pesto, the home-made mozzarella, marinara sauce ... you get the picture.

Every time we get to visit this special place, I am amazed at how every single waiter, chef, and kitchen staff intentionally pause what they're doing and greet us with a genuine smile and by name.

"Buenas noches, Señora Schumacher, Señor Schumacher! Welcome to Gustino Restaurant!"

As you enter the grand dining room, you're mesmerized by what seems like at least one hundred huge candles, all arranged into a beautiful centerpiece in the middle of the room under a soaring, dome-shaped ceiling, adorned with a stunning mural. The flickering light dresses the luxurious surroundings in a warm glow of romance.

The ambiance is magnificent. Did I mention the live saxophone player who softly plays all our favorite love songs from the eighties and nineties?

The tables are dressed in perfectly white, starched tablecloths and are set with an overwhelming amount of silverware and multiple shapes and sizes of glasses per setting. Between you and me, this is where I wished I was a little bit more educated!

Thankfully, the waiter instantly explains everything, eliminating even the slightest feeling of awkwardness or discomfort. He has the perfect blend of refined skill, class, and intuition. He is very knowledgeable and anticipates all of our needs immediately. It's almost like he can read our thoughts, and along with his assistant, is always in reach without making us feel like we're being watched. Our glasses are never empty.

The food is an experience in and of itself, and if you ever get the opportunity to vacation in Cancun, this place is a must. Bavette Al Frutti Di Mare is my absolute favorite.

When we are finished with the multiple courses, the waiter presents me with a red rose to express the restaurant's appreciation for our visit, and with that, seal another memorable experience.

As we make our way back to our room via the hotel lobby, everyone who's ever been to that restaurant knows exactly what we just experienced simply by the red rose in my hand, which undoubtedly has its very own effect.

Let me ask you:

Do you think we would go there again and tell our friends and family about this place and our experience?

You better believe it. In fact, it's not just the restaurant. The entire resort is world-class, and we have gone back to vacation there many times.

But … what does any of this have to do with building a wildly successful real estate business and strategic market domination?

Everything.

THE FOUR STAGES OF MARKET DOMINATION

1. The Host
2. The Venue
3. The Invitation
4. The Dinner Experience

As simple as this may sound, this framework summarizes my entire business model and long-term success strategy, <u>while it simultaneously explains why so many agents fail at this business</u> and end up quitting within the very first year. Before I explain what I mean, allow me to quickly define each stage for you.

1. The Host

The *Host* represents you. <u>It's who you are</u>, how you think, what you believe and expect from life. It's your goals, dreams, and aspirations, your attitude, your personality style, communication style, your level of skill, competence, and unique insight. It's your ability to ask really good questions and listen with the intent to understand, not just respond. It's your genuine desire to help people because you actually care.

2. *The Venue*

The *Venue* represents <u>your professional market presence</u>, which includes the tangibles such as your brokerage association, brand, website, social media presence and content, your marketing pieces, including your business cards, flyers, advertisements in newspapers and magazines, feature sheet and CMA report templates, signage, billboards, etc.

And it includes the intangibles such as the message you are conveying in anything and everything you put out there—intentionally or unintentionally. It's your reputation as well as the perception you create in your marketplace, in other words, <u>pre-framing what people believe about you,</u> and as a result, expect, and talk about *before* they ever meet you, and *after* they've had an interaction with you—whether that's a property inquiry via phone or email, an open house visit, or an actual buying or selling transaction. I also call that market buzz.

3. *The Invitation*

The *Invitation* represents <u>any and all activities that are intended to attract your ideal prospects and cause them to take a certain action,</u> while tastefully repelling the not so ideal ones. That includes any type of traffic you generate—paid or organic—such as your marketing campaigns on social media, print, radio, podcast, webinars, television, etc. as long as it has a clear call to action. It also includes strategic indirect *marketing campaigns* such as community events, draws, giveaways, sponsorships, and fundraisers.

4. The Dinner Experience

The *Dinner Experience* represents just that—the results that <u>your clients expect to receive, and the experience that they will remember and talk about.</u> That starts with an intentionally created and clearly outlined client journey for your buyers and sellers from start to finish, which enables you to deliver a consistent, world-class experience.

It also includes measurable and duplicable business systems and processes, as well as a support team that enables you to grow and scale your business without losing the word-class level of service that your clients have become accustomed to—**and without losing your sanity and personal life.**

To build a massively successful real estate business and **dominate your market** <u>in the FASTEST way possible,</u> all *4 Stages* have to be executed in the right scope and sequence. And even though that may sound like common sense, in reality, it's certainly not common practice.

What's the first thing *they* tell you to do when you get your license?

"Get some business cards, get a website, and start prospecting," right? *"You need to get your name out there! Do open houses every weekend, collect as many email addresses as you can, start building your database, go door-knocking, call every FSBO in town, and tell everyone you know that you're in real estate!"*

To which **anyone in their right mind** is most certainly going to respond with *"Ooh, good to know! You've never sold a house before ... I'm totally gonna entrust my biggest financial asset into your very inexperienced hands, so you can get some experience on my dime."*

Ugh.

Imagine a doctor finishing medical school, skipping the residency program, and just going straight to an independent practice. Would you trust them? I mean ... yeah, they've spent a gazillion years in school and are certainly not clueless, but are they experienced?

I believe with every fiber of my being that the #1 reason MOST agents never make it in this business is because they skip most, if not all, of *Stage 1,* randomly spend all their time, energy, and limited resources on just parts of *Stages 2 and 3,* and the result is another average *Experience*—a.k.a. *Stage 4.*

Yet nobody is excited about average, nor does anyone refer average, which is why this business model revolves around quantity and requires you to always be in 'prospecting mode', or in other words, having to reinvent the wheel over and over again.

If you ask me … that's not a business. **That is a glorified job.** A viable business is built on repeat customers who refer their friends and family, which creates goodwill, and if you do it right … at some point, *passive* cash flow.

To go back to my dinner experience story, even the most delectable food and the most mesmerizing ambiance would have been ineffective for future repeat and referral business, had the staff been average.

You've experienced it, no doubt—a waiter who's inattentive, who brings you the wrong order, forgets one of the appetizers, and when it finally gets there, *along* with your entrée … there are croutons on the salad even though you expressly requested it without.

And look, I get it. None of this is a capital offence. It's just … average.

And one thing is for sure, had the staff at Gustino treated us like that, this book wouldn't have started with that story, and chances are we would have never gone back, because there are plenty of other options out there, right?

And you know, I honestly believe that most agents don't skip *Stage 1* because they're lazy. They just genuinely have been led to believe that the mandatory licensing education was all that was needed on that level, and the rest, *you learn as you go!*

You may have thought that, too—I certainly did when I started out. The thing is that if you listen to traditional advice and do what most agents are doing and the way they're doing it, you'll get what most agents are getting, which ... I hate to sound like a broken record ... is average. And what's the average GCI of an agent in North America? 35-40 grand?

I'd rather be a barista in that case.

See, it's not hard to get a classy business card and a cool looking website these days, dress like a million bucks, and hit the streets 'prospecting' ... motivated by all the #grind and #hustle quotes on Instagram.

But **how many agents do you know that have these impressive facades,** and yet, when the rubber meets the road, and you're actually trying to do a deal with them ... it's a *DISASTER!!*

They're totally incompetent. Zero courtesy, terrible communication skills, you can't read their handwriting, they've got no clue about the difference between a term and a condition or how to draft them properly—nor where in the contract to insert them correctly for that matter! They forgot to witness a signature, missed a few initials ... and the list goes on and on.

It's like ... *Did you win your license in the lottery or somethin'?*

It's no surprise that our industry has such a bad reputation and the public thinks that agents make way too much money for the value they provide.

If you really want to build a massively successful real estate business and **dominate your market** in the FASTEST way possible, you must execute these *4 Stages* in the right scope and sequence—but also, as quickly as possible in order to build momentum—starting with *Stage 1.*

As unsexy as it sounds, you have to start with yourself! Who do you have to become in order to truly earn your community's trust as their go-to local agent? You can't give what you do not have, right?

Take a very critical look at your current level of skill, competence, and insight. Do you actually know your stuff? **Regardless of how long you've been in the business** and how many houses you've already sold—if you and I had a conversation right now, and I asked you about what the market's like in your neck of the woods ... what would you say?

How many active homes on the market? How many price reductions this past week? How many sales? How many expireds? How about compared to *LAST* week? Last month? Have you toured all these properties? Do you know why some are selling and others are sitting?

It doesn't matter whether you just got your license last month or last year—or 25 years ago. You've got to know your stuff. And I don't just mean numbers and statistics. People can get that on Google, and I don't think you want to be in competition with Google. I mean, what does any of that *MEAN* to *THEM*—your target market and target audience?

That's called insight, and nobody can compete with that. In fact, people pay a lot of money for insight.

You're in business for yourself. You decide how quickly you want to get good at this. You determine how fast you go and how quickly you get there!

Let's continue.

Do you understand human behavior, the different personality styles, and what *REALLY* causes people to act and *RE*-act the way they do? Have you mastered the art of asking the right kinds of questions that help you to quickly determine your prospects' preferred communication style and skillfully evaluate their qualification and motivation? Do you know how to adapt your selling style in such a way that your prospects feel heard and understood?

What about your attitude and your work ethic? I don't mean when things are easy, the market's hot, and sales are just happening. I mean when things are tough, when people aren't loyal, when nothing seems to be going right, and on top of that, your fellow agents are acting unethically, making decisions based on their own advantage?

That's what's going to determine your long-term success.

And not only that. **It will also determine *HOW* you will show up and execute *Stages 2, 3, and 4*.** And that changes everything.

And hey, I'm not saying that working on yourself will ever stop. After all, the saying goes that the more you know, the more you know how much you still don't know, right? But imagine the difference in the yield of your crop if you actually took the time to thoroughly and strategically prepare the ground *BEFORE* you planted the seed?

Or to use our restaurant analogy again, imagine the size of that server's tip—not only once, but time after time—if they actually took pride in their service and got the insight they needed, polished their communication and listening skills, and made you feel like you're the most important guest in the entire restaurant! It's a total game-changer, isn't it?

Imagine having an actual *step-by-step plan* for such intentional preparation and growth! Spoiler alert, it's contained on the pages ahead, and following that plan will make you an unstoppable, world-class *Host!*

Next, you must establish a distinct brand positioning in your marketplace, craft a clear marketing message that uniquely appeals to your ideal audience in your ideal market niche, and create a market presence that is excellent, consistent, and purposeful. In other words ... a world-class *Venue!*

And only once those two *Stages* are in place - in other words, the host is trained and the venue is actually ready to receive guests - is it time to send the *Invitation*. But not to just anyone and everyone ... and not how you might think!

Don't be the agent that lists the fourplex downtown, the farm up north, and the condo down south 'because it's a listing and it's your name out there'.

What do you want to be known for? Where, and why? Those are the people you invite. And whatever you decide that should look like, always remember:

Be the Flame that Attracts the Moth, Instead of Being the Lighter that Chases the Moth.

In other words, <u>your marketing should never be about you and how awesome you are.</u> It should never be about trying to persuade or convince anyone of anything. That would just add more noise to an already noisy marketplace.

Everybody says that they're the best and that *they* have the best marketing strategy and most *cutting-edge* marketing tools, which is technobabble and means *NOTHING* to a normal human being that's looking for a viable, low-risk solution to their changing lifestyle needs.

Your marketing should instead be about them. It should answer the questions they're quietly wondering about, and perhaps even discussing at the dinner table. And it should show them how you're going to help them get what they want while avoiding what they're worried about and are afraid of. More on that in a future chapter.

When *Stage 3* is up and running, things are starting to get exciting! You've prepared well, and you're ready for *Stage 4*. There's a unique buzz in the marketplace and people are starting to notice and reach out to you. Now it's time to exceed their expectations with the most amazing real estate purchase or sale experience they've ever had. From that very first phone call or email inquiry, all the way to the SOLD sign install, and everything in between should have world-class *Experience* written all over it.

To sustain that world-class level consistently, however, you're going to need the right systems and when the time is right, the right support team. And that is when your solo-preneur job turns into an actual business.

Quick Time Out:

You may have bought this book because the title intrigued you. And while you most definitely want to know *'How To Get Listings'* and some better systems in place ... **you're not quite sold on the *'Dominate Your Market'* part.**

Because, doesn't *to dominate* mean that <u>you're constantly on the road</u> and working all the time? You're never home with your family because you have to show houses every evening and weekend, you're glued to your phone, you're putting out fires all day long ... and there's this never-ending pressure?

Who wants that kind of life? *"If I can just do two-three sales a month and live a comfortable life, I'm happy!"*

I know, I just totally read your thoughts, didn't I?

It's a valid point looking in from the outside. But looking out from the inside, <u>and having been on both sides,</u> my experience has taught me that if structured and executed right, it's actually easier to dominate your market and be the #1 local agent everyone trusts and refers, and it takes a lot less time and energy than trying to do 'just two-three sales a month!' Not initially, but in the long run. The drama comes from working with the "wrong" type of people and hiring the "wrong" support staff. But if you avoid those pitfalls—which I'm going to teach you in this book —it really is *easier* to dominate your market than to just do a sale or two (or even three) a month.

How?

Well, it is my firm belief that **cream always rises to the top. NOT to dominate means** that you are NOT the most knowledgeable, competent, experienced, and connected agent in your marketplace, because if you intentionally work on becoming that agent, <u>you can't help but rise to the top!</u>

This book is about showing you how to become that agent, create the right systems and processes, build your ideal support team that will help you to sustain that high level of performance, and simultaneously **enable you to enjoy the fruit of your labor and live life on your terms.**

Now that we've laid a solid foundation and you understand the framework, let's dive into the ten skills that you absolutely must master to become a real force in your marketplace. As you may have guessed ... we're starting with YOU!

SKILL 1

MINDSET MASTERY

Whether you think you can or you think you can't,
you are right. —Henry Ford

I know, I know. Everyone seems to be talking about mindset these days. Do me a favor though, don't just skim over this chapter, **scanning the headlines,** and looking for the tactical stuff. Instead, try to read it with an open mind, and like your entire business success depended on it. Because ... it does.

You see, your mind is your most powerful tool. Every idea, every dream, and every desire or ambition you have ever had was first conceived in your mind. You may dream of breaking through in your finances and finally being able to provide for those you love, you may dream of learning a new skill, or a new language.

Perhaps, more than anything, you'd like to be able to travel and see the world, or to finally being able to buy that house on the beach.

Dreams can be so captivating. And as you literally watch them unfold on the screen of your mind—you see what could be—and for just a split second, you believe in the possibility and beauty of its fulfillment. You imagine what it would look like, feel like, and be like, and what it would mean to you and your loved ones to be in possession of that dream.

When we were kids, dreams like that were natural and frequent. We used to daydream about all the wonderful things we would be and do one day when we grew up. We dreamt of being great dancers, famous singers, actors, firefighters, policemen, or even presidents. Anything seemed possible.

Growing up in Russia, I would often look at my parents' low-quality lifestyle and huge lack of so many things, that, however hard our life conditions and circumstances seemed to be at the time, **I literally dreamt of being their hero when I'd grow up**, and one day, give them all the things they've always wanted but could never have.

I would look at the poor people on the streets, and I would day-dream of feeding them and giving them shelter and clothing. I didn't know how yet, but I was determined to do great things with my life and help a lot of people.

But then life happens, and by the time we've graduated, things changed, <u>and so did our expectations.</u> We heard the words "No," "Don't touch that," "You can't have that," and, "You can't do that," so many times that combined with our experiences, disappointing results, and setbacks, **our expectations of life**—and more impor-tantly, of ourselves—**shrunk to what's realistic and proven.**

"How are you gonna do that? Where are you gonna get the money? Who do you think you are?" You see, our upbringing, learned behavior, and our life experiences typically dictate what we think we can or cannot do. It's called conditioning. After all, it's been said that if we hear something over and over again, we eventually start to believe it. And so, instead of using this powerful tool we were given by our Creator to attract success and the things we want in life, we're actually *using* it to repel success.

We justify and defend our inability and argue for impossibility, focusing all our energy on the reasons <u>why it won't work, instead of figuring out how it could.</u>

Rather than stepping out into growth, stretching and expanding, we end up stepping back into safety ... also known as the comfort zone. Fear sets in. The fear of the unknown, the fear of failure, the fear of being rejected or exposed. We worry about all the things that could go wrong instead of focusing on all the things that could go right. And although we often don't realize it, we literally picture our defeat. We vividly imagine how we are going to mess up, fail, lose, or embarrass ourselves in front of other people, and so, sadly, <u>we give up before we even started.</u>

The sobering thing is that whether you are consciously aware of this or not, **the universal principle is that your results in life are a direct response to your most dominant thoughts and resulting emotions.**

MY VERY FIRST PROPERTY EVALUATION APPOINTMENT

I'll never forget my first ever property evaluation appointment. I don't know about you, but even though I am a fairly positive person, here's what was going on in my head that entire day while I was repeatedly fighting attacks of increased heart rate and sweaty palms.

"What in the world was I thinking to book this appointment? I have never done this before! I have absolutely no clue what I'm gonna say! How do I even know what this place is worth? What if they ask me how many houses I have already sold in this neighborhood or how long I have been in real estate? They'll never list with me if they find out that I'm just a rookie!"

Needless to say, I didn't get that listing.

If what we picture in our mind is nothing more than epic failure, and we vividly experience the fear of being rejected, then that will be the energy we exude, and people can sense that. **It becomes a self-fulfilling prophecy, and our actions simply follow our beliefs.** They always do. We will never be able to outperform our own self-image and beliefs.

In that particular story, *I had already accepted the defeat* in my mind before I even arrived at the property, and that is exactly what I got.

I fell quite a few more times after that. Lost the listings, felt so frustrated and incompetent. But the truth was that I didn't *have* any experience, so how was I supposed to feel confident and display a level of competence that would be *worthy* of anyone's trust? Valid point, isn't it?

We're getting into the practical part of the book and the step-by-step action plan shortly, I promise. However, I'm going to propose to you that before you can win any battle, you have to first win it in your mind.

And before you can win any listing, you have to win it **before you ever even meet with you seller prospects.** In fact, you have to walk in there with the attitude that they need your help so much more than you need that commission cheque, and you have to believe beyond a shadow of a doubt that not only are you best suited and qualified to serve these people on the highest level, and help them get what they want—**it is your sacred duty.**

Imagine the dramatic shift in your energy, presence, passion, and genuine care if you showed up with that kind of mindset. And imagine if you showed up like that *consistently*—even if you didn't necessarily feel like it at that particular time!

Quick Time Out: I am *NOT* talking about the *fake it till you make it* approach, nor am I saying that just thinking positively will get you anything you want in life. Although, for the record, thinking positively will get you a whole lot more in life than thinking negatively, but that's beside the point. When you begin to study Quantum Physics and the fascinating research on the Neuroplasticity of the brain, however, you will start to discover and understand that you have a whole lot more power and control over your life and business success than you may be currently realizing!

The big question is ... what's driving you?

THREE POWER QUESTIONS TO YOUR BIG WHY

Allow me to take you through a simple, yet powerful exercise that will provide you with a remarkable level of clarity.

The exercise consists of three very simple questions. However, the true power of this exercise lies in answering these questions in writing. So, why don't you grab your journal, and before we get into the *HOW* part of this book, let's talk about the *WHAT* and the *WHY!*

1. What do you really want from life? Specifically? In every area of your life, including your health, your family, your relationships, your spiritual life, your finances, your business, your contribution to the world—what is it that you really want or desire?

You see, **most people have more clarity on the things they *don't* want** in life than the things they actually do. They know that they don't want to be late, they don't want to mess up at work, they don't want to get sick, they avoid carbs because they don't want to get fat, they don't want their kids to fail in school, or have bad friends, or come home late, or get in trouble.

But, what do you actually want?

If you don't know exactly what you want from life, how are you supposed to get it? If you don't know what success <u>actually looks like</u> in all those areas I just mentioned, how will you know when you've achieved it?

Take the time to wrestle with these questions. If you were already in possession of all those things today, what would each of those areas look and feel like? Write down your answers for each category in as much detail as you possibly can. Be specific.

2. *WHY* do you want these things? Why are they important to you? Why *NOW?*

To accentuate the true power of these questions, allow me to share a quick story with you. Picture yourself on the 28th floor of a high-rise building downtown. You look out the window, and you immediately see that the building next door is on fire! It's a high-rise as well, and as you look closer, amidst all those flames and all that smoke, you suddenly notice a rope that connects all the way from your window to the burning building.

Let me ask you: Would you walk that rope to cross over to the burning building?

What a question, right? I am pretty sure you are thinking something like: *Why in the world would I?*

EXACTLY!

Now, consider this scenario:

You are on the top floor of this huge building—it's floor 28—and as you look out the window, you immediately see that the building next door is on fire! It's a high-rise as well, and as you look closer, you see something moving on the other side!

You can barely make out what it is because of all of that smoke, but as you look closer, you suddenly realize it's *YOUR* little girl, and she is desperately crying for help! Your heart is pounding! There's no way to jump across, and going down the elevator and trying to find your way back up the other building might take too long.

Then, you suddenly notice a rope that connects all the way from your window to the burning building ... where your little girl is!

Let me ask you that same question again:

Would you NOW walk that rope to cross over to the burning building?

See, when you find your *WHY*, everything shifts. Your courage shifts. Your energy shifts, your motivation, your passion, your approach, your strategies.

When you know *WHY* you are doing what you're doing, you've got a reason to jump out of bed in the morning, and you will do whatever it takes to make it work.

And that is sadly what most agents are missing. They lack true purpose. They look at the real estate business as just another thing to try and see if it might work. And when the going gets tough, and things don't work out the way they thought they would—or as quickly as they thought they would—they look at the rope, they look at the burning building, **and they look 28 stories down,** and they say:

"Why in the world would I kill myself trying to do this? It's just not for me."

This is very powerful stuff. But even though it is powerful, **how many agents will still miss the profound transformation this lesson holds?** Probably, most of them. You know why? Because they will be inspired by the concept and love the idea, but instead of actually *DOING* the work and wrestling with these questions until they get true clarity, they're just *going to do it sometime later*, which is why the urgent will continue to interrupt and distract them, and be in the way of what they really want in life.

3. If you were able to answer questions one and two, and you are having these dreams, goals, and ambitions in your heart, and you even know why you want them, chances are you've had them for a while.

So allow me to ask you, *Why haven't you already achieved them?* What's been in the way? What's been holding you back until now?

Five years from now, will that reason or excuse still be good enough?

Most of our limitations are based *not* on lack of ability or resources, but on <u>lack of belief</u>. Steve Jobs and Steve Wozniak didn't necessarily have the resources, but they had a dream and a determination to realize it. Mount Everest was impossible to climb until someone did. And the Wright Brothers ... didn't have a pilot's licence.

Your brain will always want to know the *how* <u>before</u> it will believe or approve of the *what* because it's focused on self-preservation and conserving energy.

Let's face it, you've already bought into enough bad ideas, MLMs, coaches, courses, lotions and potions, and you name it! You got burned too many times and your brilliant brain is just trying to protect you from yet another painful experience. Understandable.

But when you're led by logic only and **by what you can understand and explain,** and therefore, project what's possible in the future based on what happened or has been proven in the past, you are in danger of shutting out growth and expansion from your life. After all, "If you want something you have never had, you must be willing to do something you have never done." One of my favorite quotes by Thomas Jefferson.

If your decisions in life and business are limited by your current understanding of the *how,* getting stuck is pretty much inevitable. If your focus is on the *what,* however, and that *what* is fuelled and driven by a clear and very compelling *why,* your mind has the nearly infinite power to *figure out the how.* And you might be thinking, *Ya, Alina, easy for you to say. You have no idea what I'm up against in my market!*

Try me!

THE AGENT WITH ALL THE FOR SALE SIGNS IN TOWN

I remember just like it was yesterday. I finally had my license and was so excited to serve my marketplace! But it seemed like no matter where I turned, *her* directional signs were on the street corner, and whatever property I went to preview, *her* FOR SALE sign was at the end of the driveway. She owned the market. **She was literally everywhere, and everybody knew her.**

She was born and raised in the area ... I was not. She spoke perfect English and understood the community culture and its local nuances ... I was having a hard time understanding even the simplest things people were asking me.

She knew the market and had all these years of experience ... I didn't. She was more mature in age, which in my mind, meant that she instantly looked more competent and trustworthy ... I looked like I had just graduated from high school.

She had a fancy SUV ... I was driving our family van and often had my three munchkins with me in the backseat because I didn't have a babysitter. In fact, I remember this one time, pulling into the driveway to show one of her listings, not realizing that she'd be there, showing it to her clients at the same time. And **I remember feeling so embarrassed and guilty.** What kind of a mother would drag her little ones to work like that and leave them in the car by themselves, telling them to sit quietly and duck should this lady walk by the van while Mommy was showing the house?

Ugh.

She was a giant ... I was a complete unknown. She was LAPS ahead of me.

How do you ever compete with that?

Oh, that brain and that *how* question again. <u>Seriously, though, how DO you compete with that?</u>

To follow my own advice, which took me years and a gazillion detours to figure out, I learned to ask a different kind of question. And that question changed everything for me, and I hope it does the same for you.

Who do you have to become to truly earn your community's trust? What skills would you need to acquire and display in order to become the #1 local agent in your marketplace?

Once you start directing your energy and focus towards questions like that, everything shifts, and your path becomes clear.

It doesn't matter where you start. It doesn't matter what you think you have or don't have. It doesn't matter how inadequate or small you may feel right now, nor how many giants may be occupying the Promised Land. None of that matters.

Remember, Cream Always Rises to the Top!

Once your thoughts and beliefs shift to that truth, there is no more competition for you! Because now it's up to you to **get so good at what you do, that your competition becomes irrelevant.**

The good news is that you're on the right track. You are a person of growth, and the very fact that you are reading this book shows me that you're hungry to learn and ready for more. More freedom, more meaning, more impact—but there's a huge danger, and that danger is called *overwhelm.*

Everywhere you go, there seems to be an ad with somebody promoting yet another webinar, **trying to sell you another real estate course, another coaching program, and another must-have, fancy lead generation CRM.** Everybody claims to have the answer.

In fact, when you google the term, "real estate coach," you get a whole bunch of search results of coaches who all claim to be *"The #1 Real Estate Coach in North America."* Not sure how that works. Everybody promises results. And don't get me wrong … I am not saying that their stuff is bad or doesn't work.

What I am saying is that there are many different approaches and business models, and it's perfectly natural to want to research, compare, and find the best solution *for you*. Probably no different than what your seller prospects are doing when they're shopping for an agent, right?

But when you get stuck in research mode and just <u>follow every coach and approach</u> under the sun **because you're afraid of missing out** (FOMO), overwhelm is inevitable.

Find someone who already has the results you want, and **if their approach resonates with you,** <u>go unfollow all the others</u> to eliminate distraction, and commit to doing exactly what they're teaching you to do.

Sustained focus really is the new superpower and it results from a strong mindset.

Let's run a few more practice laps as we're continuing to work on *Stage 1* of the Market Domination Plan, and let's talk about understanding human behavior and the power of asking great questions in the next few chapters.

To access your FREE book bonuses go to:
www.AlinaSchumacher.com/bookbonuses

SKILL 2

THE ART OF UNDERSTANDING HUMAN BEHAVIOR

Someone once said that business would be easy if it weren't for the people. Have you ever felt that way? People can be pretty *interesting,* and yet, the profession you have chosen doesn't just revolve around people, it revolves around what is likely the highest financial asset they possess, and **you know what else they say ... you really get to know people when it's about their money!**

The ability to understand people, what drives them, and what causes them to act and *react* the way they do is one of the most important skills you will ever develop. Because even though we're all unique and different, we are predictably different. And knowing how to quickly determine someone's potential behavioral and communication style and being able to adapt your own communication style accordingly will not only help you to connect and earn their trust in the quickest way possible, it'll enable you to customize the entire *experience* in a way that will be most meaningful and relevant to *them,* and with that, create lifetime clients who refer their friends and family.

There are quite a few different personality profiling tools on the market. The two that I found most helpful, however, are the DISC and the Enneagram. The DISC is perfect for professional purposes because it's relatively easy and quick to apply, even to people you have never met before—if you know the clues.

The Enneagram is more of a personal journey, and the reason I think it's important is because it helps you to understand your*self* on a much deeper level, and with that, be so much more effective in understanding and adapting to others. My goal in this chapter is to give you a brief overview on the DISC and then recommend a few great books that will help you to dive deeper and master this skill.

Question For You...

Have you ever met someone where, within just minutes of talking to them, you felt like you've known each other forever? You can't believe how many things you have in common—they think like you, they have the same interests, and they totally get your humor. It's like two old friends that have a lifetime of catching up to do! Best of all, you don't need a filter and can just be yourself.

Then, there are people where you definitely need to work a little harder on what you say and how you say it to make sure they don't misunderstand you. You think and process things differently, which is fine, it just requires special effort.

And then, off and on, you meet people that just crawl under your skin, and everything about them repels you! Why is that?

Everyone has a story, and I bet if you and I had a chance to hear the stories of some of those *more difficult* people in our lives, it would explain a few things. There's a reason why we are the way we are—we explored that in the previous chapter. What we all have in common, however, is that we instinctively move towards the things that bring us pleasure and make us feel good, and we instinctively move away from the things that cause us pain. Our brains are wired that way.

Having said that, the motivation to avoid pain (loss, embarrassment, criticism, etc.) is far greater than the motivation to gain pleasure. **That pain looks different for each behavioral style,** and over time, we develop certain traits or skills that help us cope and to an extent, "control" and wherever possible, avoid that particular pain.

For example:

A behavioral style that is short and to the point, decisive, driven, very task and results-oriented can come across as quite dominating, fairly direct, and even blunt, or brash sometimes because their *greatest fear is the fear of being disrespected and taken advantage of.* So in order to compensate for that, they try to be in control of a situation (or people) whenever possible—whether that is at work or at home.

=> In the DISC system, this is the *D-style,* which stands for DOMINANT. About 3% of the population are *High D.*

The personality style of that social butterfly we all know and often admire is that they are very open and outgoing, charming, inspiring, creative, impulsive, emotional, flattering, and chatty, giving away way too much personal information because their greatest desire is to be accepted—which is why they care so much about what people think of them. Their greatest fear is to be rejected by people, *which is why they work so hard on trying to be LIKED by everyone.*

=> In the DISC system, this is the *I-style,* which stands for INFLUENTIAL or INSPIRING. About 17% of the population are *High I.* (Personally, I think that whoever came up with the concept of *likes* on social media, clearly must have been a *High I…*)

Then, there is the style that is steady, dependable, loyal, and happy to be with people, without having to be the center of attention. This style doesn't express feelings or opinions openly, unless they are being asked—even though they certainly have one. They dread change with every fiber of their being and need a lot of time to think about things and prepare in advance. Making a decision is usually a process because they first have to consider how their decision is going to impact all the other people in their lives. Their greatest fear is their loss of security, which explains why they are drawn towards a life that is steady and predictable, where they know exactly what to expect. This style represents the majority of the population—about 69%—which should be a clue.

=> In the DISC system, this is the *S-style,* which stands for STEADY.

Lastly, we have the critical thinkers, spreadsheet-loving loyalists, and *walking encyclopedias*, who can come across as cool and reserved at first because they need time to warm up and develop trust. They pride themselves in being detail-oriented to a fault, and their worst nightmare is someone who questions their work and actually *finds* a mistake. They hate being wrong, and they hate admitting it. Therefore, in order to avoid that pain, don't expect them to make any fast decisions or give you an answer right away. They need a few days to research and make sure they make the right decision, or their answer is correct and indisputable.

=> In the DISC system, this is the *C-style,* which stands for COMPLIANT or CONSCIENTIOUS. About 11% of the population are *High C.*

Imagine the power of being able to analyze the communication and behavioral clues of each style quickly and adjust your communication style in such a way where you can skillfully, yet ethically **alleviate your prospects most dominant pain or fear**, and make them feel comfortable, respected, and understood! Do you think that would give you a significant edge, and help you build rapport and trust with your prospects quicker than ever? You better believe it.

That, right there, is my secret sauce in sales.

To Quickly Determine the Potential Behavioural Style of a Person, Start by Looking at the Following Two Indicators:

1. Is this person more people or task-oriented?
2. Is this person open or more closed when it comes to expressing their feelings and opinions?

If you have someone who is task-oriented and open, you're dealing with a High D.

If you have someone who is people-oriented and open, you're dealing with a High I.

If you have someone who is people-oriented and closed, you're dealing with a High S.

If you have someone who is task-oriented and closed, you're dealing with a High C.

Imagine someone with a very clear vision of what they want and able to make fast decisions trying to sell to someone who needs a detailed spreadsheet and an extra day or two to think about it because that's just how they're wired! No amount of pressure is going to accelerate the decision-making process. In fact, pressure will have the opposite effect.

A *High C* and *S* need time to process things, and they usually need to sleep on it, talk to their family, and consider the pros and cons before they're going to make a decision. **Pressuring them will knock the breath right out of your sale.** Understanding how to give them space and follow up correctly, however, will make all the difference.

If you turn those examples around, they'd be just as dysfunctional because if a *High D* has already DECIDED to buy and just wants to know where to sign, but the *High C* continues to sell, because they haven't finished explaining the fine print yet, the *High D* is going to feel annoyed and frustrated.

HOW TO APPLY THIS IN YOUR NEXT PROPERTY EVALUATION APPOINTMENT

Let's imagine that you're about to head into a home evaluation appointment and meet with a new home seller prospect. What are the clues that you should be paying attention to? What kind of questions could you be asking them to quickly discover their potential personality style and adapt your communication style accordingly?

Personally, I would start looking for those clues even *before* I meet with a new prospect. You can tell a lot about someone's personality style simply by observing how they communicate on the phone and in their emails.

While a *High D* will get straight to the point and **likely omit any polite remarks, questions, and pleasantries,** the *High-S* and *High-I's* writing style will be more friendly, with a whole lot more personal detail, and likely an apology for any potential inconvenience.

The *High-C's* emails will be long and detailed, correct to a T, spellchecked, and formatted with bullet points and numbers for easier future reference.

When you meet with your prospects face-to-face, you can find out a lot about their potential personality style just by looking at the surroundings. Is it cluttered and somewhat messy? Or does everything match perfectly and is organized to sheer perfection? Are the walls simply white or is there a lot of color and texture? Are there a lot of family photographs on the walls? Are there any achievement awards, degrees, and diploma frames on the walls?

All of that is telling you something.

Having said that, **we all know that opposites attract,** and chances are if you're dealing with a couple, you're dealing with two completely opposite styles. So the house might be minimalistic, neat, and clean, but when you look in the garage ... *it's being worked in* and there's stuff everywhere! (Because it's better to have it and not to need it than to need it and not to have it—which is the life motto of about 69% of the population.) Or, perhaps, the house is a little cluttered, but the garage is perfectly organized with pegboard walls, hooks, bins, and all tools neatly hung by shape and size. Those are all clues.

To get some great insight even faster, a question I'd always ask my home seller prospects as they were showing me through the home was what they do for a living. It's an easy question to slide in after you've done some small talk, established some trust, and are moving on to the next room. And the answer will give you that **insight** pretty much instantly. It's helpful to have that information later in the process as you coordinate showings, anyways.

High D

A *High D* will give a short and a bottom-line answer, and they typically won't engage in too much small talk because they like to separate business and personal, and are focused on the task at hand—which is to show you the house and get an idea as to what it's worth.

They will typically either **own a business, or have some sort of leadership, management, or sales position where they have a lot of control and freedom.** A *High D* expects you to be focused on the task, know your stuff, and communicate clearly and to the point—without beating around the bush. If you're a *High I* or a *High S*, you might think that being personable will somehow help you to build rapport. But with a *High D,* that'll usually have the opposite effect.

Once you've prepared your CMA report, be sure to give them a brief summary of the most pertinent details because that's the only thing a *High D* really cares about. And don't be afraid to ask for the order—they'll respect you for that.

By the way, in the animal world, a *High D* personality would most likely resemble a lion. In other words, respect their territory and understand they expect to be the center of attention.

High I

When you ask a *High I* what they do for a living ... you better have some time. Because they will tell you what they currently do and why they decided to do it, how long they have been doing it, plus, what they used to do before that. A *High I's* profession will usually be something where they can be creative with as little rules and boundaries as possible, while being with people. **In other words, these are the artists, news reporters, hair stylists, and of course ... salespeople.**

Their home might look tidy on the surface, but when you open the kitchen drawers or the closet doors ... well, you know. Expect a lot of color and texture, unique art, and a cosy atmosphere.

By the way, when you ask a *High I* about home improvements, make sure to verify the information before you publish it because they often tend to exaggerate the dates or how much they paid for something. Not intentionally ... just that details aren't really their thing. Besides, they are trying to impress you and make you like them, remember? In fact, a *High I* will only do business with you if they first feel a connection and that you really are a kindred spirit.

You'll quickly notice that a *High I* is very self-promoting and absolutely loves talking about themselves. Granted, most people do, but *High I's* especially. They might ask you about your family, but as soon as you've finished your sentence, they'll probably take over and tell you all about theirs.

They might even show you a picture of the grandkids. So, if you want to earn their business, take the time to listen, socialize a little, and show them how impressed you are with their home as well as their achievements. If you are a *High D,* I saw you cringing!!

In the animal world, a *High I* personality would most likely resemble an otter.

High S

When you ask a *High S* what they do for a living, you'll get a warm, and usually very humble answer, and it'll be something that has to do with serving or supporting other people. **High Ss make wonderful nurses, vets, social workers, counsellors, receptionists, and personal assistants** because they are calm, nurturing, people-oriented, and very understanding.

They'll make you feel welcome, they might offer you some coffee, and they'll be very open to your suggestions and carefully listen to what you have to say. You will typically find a lot of memorabilia throughout their home, and of course, many family pictures on the walls because *High Ss* are all about people, and more specifically, about family.

Since they are so nice and seriously dislike any type of pressure or conflict, they're constantly trying to please everyone. In fact, they actually feel responsible for making sure that everyone is happy.

Once they've spoken with two or three agents regarding the selling process, they may feel torn and have a hard time making a decision because they don't want to disappoint anyone.

Since they dislike uncertainty and change and can be indecisive, you've got to engage a different approach with them than you would with a *High D*—who is decisive, or a *High I*—who is spontaneous and impulsive. In fact, you will make a big mistake if you ask a *High S* for a commitment right away. (Remember, that's 69% of the population!) Ask for permission to follow up tomorrow and focus your follow up on any potentially unanswered or new questions they may be having.

In the animal world, a *High-S* personality would most likely resemble a golden retriever.

High C

And finally, the *High-C* style. These people can usually come across as reserved and cool at first—perhaps even a bit skeptical. They usually need quite a bit of time to open up and develop trust. In fact, these evaluation appointments generally last longer than usual because *High-C* people are very detail-oriented, and if you want their business—do not to rush them. In other words, these are not your drive-by kind of appointments.

High-C style people make reliable **bookkeepers, accountants, bankers, engineers, computer nerds—in other words, anything that has to do with tasks, numbers, and a lot of detail.**

They are more about order and practicality than the latest and greatest trends, and you can expect their homes to be tidy, and their closets perfectly organized—with all shoes pointing North. They will probably have a spreadsheet worth of questions for you, in fact, you shouldn't be surprised if they actually write down all your responses so they can reference the information later.

They'll also have a spreadsheet with all the home upgrades information, complete with the exact expense amounts, the supporting bills, and the remaining warranties. If you intend to gain their trust, be extremely well prepared and openly acknowledge their thoroughness.

In the animal world, a *High-C* personality style would most likely resemble a beaver.

Are You Getting the Power of This?

When I first discovered all this back in 2006, I was beyond fascinated. It explained so much! Imagine <u>how many deals you have probably already lost or potentially missed out on</u> because, even though you may have known about this concept for a while, you never really knew how to actually apply it?

Knowing and understanding this information will not only help you to become the most effective salesperson, it'll also help you with your personal relationships. And oftentimes, <u>when it seems like you're getting a lot of resistance from your spouse</u> or partner, it's not that they don't like your dreams or reject ideas, **it's just that their tolerance for risk and change is a lot lower than yours,** and they want to make sure their sense of safety and security isn't jeopardized.

And if you take the time to listen, understand, and acknowledge their concerns, show them that you have an actual plan, and that you've taken the time to think things through—they are going to be happy to support you.

Obviously, I am just scratching the surface here because in reality, <u>no human being could ever be limited to just one exclusive type.</u>

Instead, most people have one dominant style plus different levels of the other three styles.

In addition to that, we usually portray a different type of behavior in public or in a professional setting than we do at home, in a more relaxed environment. And when you add self-awareness as well as that intentional growth mindset that we talked about in the beginning of this book, you open the doors to maturity and balance—which is the ultimate goal for each behavioral style.

Working on mastering this skill was a **significant reason for my rapid success** because it enabled me to understand, adapt, and convert my prospects far more effectively, earn their repeat and referral business, and as a result, focus on quality instead of having to chase quantity.

Obviously, this is not about manipulation. It's about ethical influence and about serving your clients the way they want to be served. The best way to get started would probably be by starting to understand yourself before you try to understand others. PeopleKeys. com is a great resource for that and has a comprehensive online test as well as some really great, free information.

Once you've completed the test, you will get a customized report, and even though it may look a little overwhelming at first, make sure to not just glance over it. Take a few minutes to actually read through it—**even if at first you don't like what it says.**

When you're ready to go deeper, I would highly recommend diving into the Enneagram, which is a truly profound journey of self-discovery where it's not so much about *what* you do - but *why* you're doing it. It will no doubt be filled with many epiphanies and perhaps even life-changing revelations. It did that and more for me.

The books that I've found most helpful are by Ian Morgan Cron and Suzanne Stabile, *The Road Back To You*, and Beatrice Chestnut, *The Complete Enneagram*.

The breakthroughs and freedom you will gain from this insight alone could change everything for you.

SKILL 3

THE POWER OF A GREAT QUESTION

The year was early 2000, and I was a young, stay-at-home mom with a toddler and a six-month-old. It must have been around noon, because I was about to put my babies down for their afternoon nap when suddenly the doorbell rang. It was a vacuum salesman, and he was selling one of those very expensive and super fancy Vorwerk vacuum cleaners that I had heard of and knew that we couldn't afford anyway.

As I was cringing on the inside, wondering how I might be able to elegantly shake him off, he did something I did not expect. With just a few simple questions, he not only interrupted my thought pattern and changed the state of my mind—he changed my perception of him as well as my willingness to listen to what he had to say.

"Good afternoon, ma'am! May I ask, do you have any carpets in your home?" To which I replied, *"Yes, I do!"*

"May I ask, how often do you typically vacuum them?" And you might think I'm crazy, but I actually vacuum every single day. Sometimes twice.

So, he asked, *"How confident are you that your carpets are actually clean?"*

"Uhm ... Excuse me?" I raised my eyebrows, and before I was able to say anything, he asked if I would permit him to DEMONSTRATE to me how much dust was actually still in my carpet.

Talk About Letting in a Stranger ... But He Had My Curiosity!

So, he came in, and noticing I had two little ones, he commented on how wonderful it was to see a young family with beautiful children. Smart man. He took out his fancy machine, put in a brand-new dust bag right in front of my eyes, and then he vacuumed about eight-ten SF of my wall-to-wall living room carpet.

You already know what happened next, but as a young Mom ... I was shocked!

He pulled out the dust bag and showed me about two handfuls of solid dust that he had just gotten out of my carpet and then proceeded to explain what that dust did to the health of my family. Can't argue with facts. Obviously, he also showed me a few pictures of grossly scary dust mites, and needless to say, I was horrified.

The *SALE WAS MADE,* however, when he concluded with the fact that my little ones were crawling around and playing on that carpet ... and breathing in all that dust and those disgusting looking dust mites every single day. And he said it with such genuine care and concern—he had me.

He couldn't have known that I had literally just vacuumed that rug an hour or so ago. Long story short, I asked him to come back in the evening when my husband was home, and <u>we bought a vacuum cleaner that night.</u>

To say that this guy was the most genius, non-salesy salesman I've ever met would be an understatement.

Not only was he able to instantly capture my attention by asking a few simple, but very effective questions, but he also added value to me, educated, and triggered a certain emotion within me. Then, he didn't pressure me into making a decision right away. In fact, **he didn't even ask for the order.** The process went perfectly natural.

And yet, one thing is for sure... <u>That morning, I didn't get up with the intention of buying an expensive vacuum cleaner!</u>

And had he rung the doorbell and asked if I'm interested in buying the world's most awesome, new vacuum cleaner, you can bet a billion dollars I would've said, "*Heck, NO!*"

My frame of mind and my two main objections would have been:

1. I already have one.
2. I can't afford it.

Every single day, however, I was passionate about protecting my children and creating a safe environment where they could grow up as healthy and vibrantly as possible. And *THAT* is the conversation this guy entered in my mind —starting with a simple question!

THE SECRET

The secret that isn't really a secret is that words really do matter. **What you say and *how* you say it really does make all the difference** in your ability to effectively attract and convert your ideal prospects and earn their future repeat and referral business—but not how you might think.

I can't tell you how many agents I have trained over the past twelve years who were all paralyzed by this fear of: "*I don't know what to say. What if they ask me this? And how do I respond if they say that ... without sounding like a rookie?*"

These are similar to the questions I was asking myself back in Chapter One when we were talking about mindset mastery, remember?

And I totally get it. Because **we earn trust in one-dollar bills and spend it in one hundred-dollar bills,** and just a single 'wrong' word or sentence ... and things can go south pretty quickly.

But instead of memorizing a gazillion different sales scripts and objection-handing techniques like most agents are trying to do, here's the paradigm shift that is going to eliminate these, *"I don't know what to say"* fears and uncertainties you may have for as long as you live.

Ready?

When you are in *selling* mode, your frame of mind is all about trying to convince and persuade someone why your product or service is better than anyone else's and why they should work with you. So, then, naturally, the more compelling your presentation and value proposition, the faster they will hopefully sign the dotted line, right?

When you are in *serving and consulting* mode, however, **you can't really prescribe a solution unless you understand the problem!**

Imagine a doctor stressing out over what to say when a patient walks into their office. Ludicrous, right? They don't even know yet what the problem is. Why would they <u>need</u> to say *ANYTHING* or worry about it for that matter?

The same applies for you.

Next time you are out on a property evaluation appointment, instead of worrying about what you're going to say, let's ask some great questions and then just listen—and I mean really listen with the intent to understand.

For example, *"If you don't mind my asking, what's most important to you and your family in selling your home?"*

Most people are going to want as much money as possible, as quickly as possible, so they can get to their new place as quickly as possible—we already know that. By answering the question out loud, however, they are actually getting a higher level of clarity on their goals and will subconsciously associate that with you.

... *"That agent was different, they were really helpful, actually!"*

A few more simple, yet very powerful questions are:

"Are you excited to move? What's the one thing you're gonna miss the most about this place? Anything you're NOT gonna miss at all ... and are happy to part with?"

And obviously, each of these questions are going to open the door to more questions. If something is unclear, **don't pretend like you're getting it.**

Authenticity always wins. Just ask, *"How so? Could you help me understand that better?"* People will totally appreciate that!

See, most agents don't actually listen. They *look* like they are listening on the outside, but in their head, they're already planning what they're going to say next.

Once you fully understand their goals, the problem(s) they're trying to solve, as well as all the terms and conditions around it—then, and only then are you able to prescribe the best and most viable solution that will solve that problem and help them get the results they want.

Whether you walk into a listing presentation appointment, talk with an Open House prospect, or negotiate an offer on behalf of a buyer or seller—**you're in the business of solving problems and offering solutions**—a.k.a. delivering results.

It's not about you, or about what you say, **and how clever you sound saying it.**

It's about whether or not you understand the problem and are able to generate the most viable, profitable, and effective solution—<u>FOR THEM.</u> That requires an entirely different way of thinking!

ANOTHER QUICK STORY

A few years ago, I had the privilege of serving a pastor of a larger, non-denominational church, who, as it turned out, was quite worried about being *judged* by his congregation, which, as a result, heavily influenced his entire belief system on the type of home he *should* be buying.

He and his beautiful wife had a nice and very comfortable home in the city (almost too nice for some of his congregational members, if you know what I mean—which is probably what led to his limiting beliefs), and they were now seeking the privacy and quiet of the country. They figured that if they bought a modest home in the country, then they could still afford a small cottage by the lake, which would provide the private get-away they were seeking. After listening to them for a while and asking a few, slightly uncomfortable, questions, they realized their self-imposed limitations and the mental cage they had built for themselves.

They decided to purchase an absolutely stunning home in the country that was very well within their budget and just happened to come with an additional small pioneer log cottage—complete with a kitchenette, wood stove, and a built-in bed in the attic!

All this was situated on five of the most glorious acres you ever saw, tucked in the most peaceful pine forest, and surrounded by a beautiful wildflower meadow. No word of an exaggeration—talk about a dream come true for a sermon-writer. You cannot imagine their level of gratitude and happiness with their new home. Would it have happened if I hadn't taken the time to ask questions, understand the underlying motivation, and help them make the decision that was right *for them*? Not in this case.

Guiding your clients into a deeper and higher sense of awareness is hands down the most powerful way of setting yourself apart from other agents.

More importantly, it is your SACRED duty to serve on that level.

In fact, while other agents will be regurgitating canned sales talks and the 47 different objection-handling techniques they found on YouTube, trying to get a signature TODAY—you are focusing on genuine care and human connection first.

And that can only happen if you put your own agenda aside, ask great questions, listen with the intent to understand, and then prescribe the shortest and most efficient path to get the results they want.

SKILL 4

FOCUSED INTENSITY ...
WITH A PLAN

If you want to take over your local market, even if there already is an agent dominating it at this time, you need a plan. **This chapter contains that plan,** and following these strategies to a *T* will help you accomplish that in the fastest and most effective way.

Once you have decided on the geographical area that you want to establish in (ideally about 400-600 homes), let's get to know that market area better than anyone else. This may sound too simplistic, but you literally have to know everything about it. Every street, backroad, and shortcut, neighborhood demographics, local features, pros and cons, the development proposals and future growth plans, current zoning regulations, restrictions, amenities, school catchment areas, etc.

Meet with your local city/municipality development officer. Ask questions. Ask for insight. Start attending the local town or municipal planning meetings but be careful not to get sucked into some political citizen agendas. You just want to learn about upcoming projects and the local development situation, as well as understand the processes. And even though you don't have to go to every single meeting, you'd be surprised how much you can learn there about the community and all that it entails.

I developed a good relationship with our town's planning officer and reeve, which ended up being a great help in my business and resulted in multiple property listings where I represented the municipality as my client, which added to my credibility and social proof.

Whether you are going to be showing homes to out-of-town buyers or the locals—your extra-mile service and insider knowledge will come in handy in building trust and rapport ultra-fast, while helping to connect the dots for people.

INVENTORY KNOWLEDGE

Now that you have a pretty good overview of the market area you want to establish in, free up some time in your schedule, and let's tour every single active listing that is currently on the market. This strategy right here—as simple as it sounds—is market domination and confidence-building on steroids.

Do it even if you aren't brand new, and already have some forward momentum—this will 10X it!

Set up showing routes for yourself by dividing all your market inventory into individual neighborhood pockets and into a manageable amount of homes that you can tour per day, depending on current market inventory.

The very best—even though at first, somewhat tedious, but oh so effective insider strategy—*especially if you are brand new,* OR *have recently moved to a new city* is this: Get yourself a new binder and print out a detailed MLS info sheet for every single property that's currently for sale in your target market area.

Oh, I know that you've got all that online, but you want to be doing the 1% kind of stuff, right?

This is going to be your weapon of mass-conversion in the future, one that very few if any agents will have, and that'll make you look and sound like *"you've been doing this forever."*

As you tour each of those properties, take notes on the following:

- How does the property show on a scale from 1-10?
- What's the layout and overall functionality like?
- Does it need updating?
- How clean is it on a scale from 1-10?
- How does it smell? (Yes, I'm serious—clean, musty smoky, pet odor, you get the point.)
- What are the pros and cons of the property? Anything else that stands out?
- What are the pros and cons of the location?

In addition to that, let's answer the following three questions:

1. If this was your listing, what would you have priced it at?
2. What tips would you give these homeowners to make their home show even better and sell faster if they were *your* clients?
3. Why might this home not have sold yet?

If you're new to this, the first few properties are going to be a little difficult, no doubt. However, imagine your level of confidence, insight, and competence by the time you're on the 25th one! This is powerful stuff.

BUT WHAT IF WE TOOK THIS TO A WHOLE NEW LEVEL?

How?

What if you actually *hand-wrote* a thank you note for every single home you previewed, and attached one of those world-class, can't-throw-away-kind-of-quality business cards to it? (I love moo.com)

Just make sure that it's a generic thank you note (*not branded*) because your goal is to express genuine gratitude to the homeowners for allowing you to preview or show their home—*NOT* to make it look like you have an agenda.

When you write the note, add something specific that you especially appreciated about their home … and that's it. No ulterior motives.

Just a small token of appreciation, **because if you've ever sold a house,** you know how much time and effort goes into getting it ready for a showing, right? Let's acknowledge that.

Now, if saying thank you to the homeowner threatens the listing agent … let's just say that they've got bigger problems.

Between you and me, though, I've got students all over North America, and I have *NEVER* heard anyone complaining about this. In fact, some told me that even the listing agent thought that it was a nice gesture.

The bottom line is we never get a second chance to make a great first impression, and while so many agents will often **show up late, stay longer,** accidentally lock the mudroom door to the garage … and mysteriously leave the patio doors unlocked, plus forget to turn off some lights—you displayed what world-class service really looks like.

I cannot even begin to tell you how many times I'd get the call to list a property that had expired with the other agent because the homeowners were so impressed with my drive and dedication to excellence. And it all started with **paying attention to those small details that most agents don't have time for.**

Hang on to that binder after you're finished touring all those homes and taking all those notes. We will need it again in the very near future.

Let's move on.

THE RED TAPE MASTERY

I can only imagine the expression on your face right now...

It gets better, I promise. I am talking about your ability to know and really understand every single document that you will encounter in your capacity as an agent, representing your clients in the purchase and/or sale of their home.

When you took the real estate course, you learned **how to 'fill in the blanks',** and I don't know about you, but in my course books, the sample contracts had more *NONE*'s and *NIL*'s than anything else.

And as you already might have guessed, I've never been one to just blindly follow instructions and *do it because they said so*. I like to know WHY. I like to understand things. **Why NONE?** Why NIL? Why does it not apply?

A memorable brand, a catchy slogan, and beautifully printed marketing pieces will only get you so far. And while they might open some doors, <u>if you're even just slightly insecure or simply</u>

<u>unsure about something</u>, all that trust that you worked so hard to establish ... will quickly be lost again.

If you don't fully understand the contract language and what every single paragraph, sentence, and word—<u>or the lack thereof</u>—means as it relates to each party to the contract, how could you ever represent your clients' *best* interests?

Chances are you're bound to miss something, and cause totally avoidable stress and potentially serious consequences for your clients, while **throwing away tens, if not hundreds of thousands of dollars** in future repeat and referral business.

Let that sink in for a moment.

> *When opportunity comes, it's too late to prepare.*
> —*UCLA Coach, John Wooden*

So, let's prepare now, and when we move on to *Stage 3,* which is sending the *Invitation*—or in other words, start driving traffic— you're ready to perform and demonstrate your level of insight and competence in a confident manner. If English is your native language, you're already lapse ahead of me!

Since English is my fourth language, I had to work extra hard on this skill.

I read and re-read every single contract and legal form I could find at the office, until I <u>not only</u> comprehended the contract language, but actually understood the true implication of every single *word*—for the seller, the buyer, *AND* myself, the representing agent.

I practiced filling out contracts, and I honed my skills of well-written buyer vs. seller targeted terms and conditions, depending on whom I represented.

I wanted to be able to demonstrate a high level of competence to my clients and assure them that they were indeed in the best of hands—even though I did look like I had just graduated from high school at that time. But who cares if you actually know your stuff, right?

Every athlete who is serious about winning, practices every single move every single day.

You and I should, too. Besides, it comes in really handy when you're sitting across the table from that anxious first-time homebuyer couple that has a cranky baby, a very tight budget ... and is really nervous about making a mistake. *What a privilege to serve and make this experience as flawless and positive as possible for them!*

You Are in the Driver's Seat; You Determine How Fast You Go!

So, are you ready to do this?

If so, get yourself a copy of every legal form and document you can find at the office, **make a huge pot of coffee,** and then let's read each form at least <u>100 times</u>—or until you have reached a true level of mastery. If there's something you don't understand, that's to be expected.

However, it's on you to seek the necessary advice to truly comprehend things if you're going to take your responsibility of protecting your clients' best interests seriously.

Personally, I asked my broker to help me understand things, to which his response was: *"That's what they have lawyers for!"* And even though he was a really nice guy, you can probably imagine *that* kind of answer was not satisfactory to me.

So I contacted my lawyer, and he was kind enough to not only meet with me multiple times and answer all my questions, but he went the extra mile and based on a few actual deals he was working on (with all private information blacked out of course), showed me all the potential loopholes and how each of those contracts would stand up in court if challenged—based on how they were completed by the representing agents.

Ugh.

Next, I took all that knowledge and went back to studying. <u>They say that if you want to learn, learn by teaching,</u> and since I'd eventually have to be able to not only fill out the documents correctly, but also present them to the respective parties—**without putting them to sleep**—I paraphrased every single paragraph to the level where I could easily explain it to a fifth-grader.

Besides meeting with my lawyer, I also met with a few mortgage brokers and multiple local builders to get some more special insight.

In fact, if you want to combine an amazing learning experience with adding massive value to the person you're learning from, invite them to a Lunch'n Learn and ask them some really great questions!

And if you're really brave, I'd also find a few successful and reputable agents who aren't a direct competitor (I know what you're thinking ... do it anyway), and ask to buy them lunch as well!

What kind of questions should you ask?

Let's start with the Agent Lunch'n Learn:

"How long have you been in Real Estate now? And if I may ask, what did you do before that?"

"What do you enjoy most about this business?"

"What's your least favorite thing about the industry, and why?"

"What has been the most painful lesson you've ever learned in this business?"

"I am obviously new to this and I am looking to learn from the best, and so ... if you could give me your very best insight on what I should do as a brand-new agent, what would it be?"

"If you had to start all over again, knowing what you know now ... what are the one or two things you'd focus on most in your business, and what are the things you'd never do again?"

When you meet with a Lawyer/Mortgage Broker:

"What common mistakes do you see agents make that I should be aware of?"

"What is most frustrating to you in dealing with agents and what specifically can I do better?"

"What would be your best piece of advice to a brand-new agent?"

"What, in your experience, are the typical mistakes buyers make when they're looking to get the best deal on financing?"

When you meet with a local Builder:

"How long have you been working in this area?"

"Do you build spec homes only or custom as well?"

"What do you love most about this business, and if I may ask, why did you decide to start your own company?"

"If you don't mind sharing, what are your plans and where do you see yourself 3-5 years from now?"

"Do you cooperate with outside agents, and if so, what is the procedure if I had a client who'd like to build a custom home? (Get info on available building lots, plans, layouts, timelines, your involvement requirements as the representing agent, and what type of compensation they offer.)

"If you had a magic wand and could change ANYTHING about your business right now—what would it be?"

I can't even begin to describe to you <u>how much insight you will gain</u> from this experience by asking these simple questions.

Make sure to come really well prepared, have a pen and notepad ready to take notes, respect their time, and pick up the bill at the end of the meeting. You will no doubt make a lasting impression.

To seal it, mail them a hand-written thank you note the next day, expressing your gratitude for their time and wisdom.

Your level of professionalism, excellence, and even experience doesn't depend on how long you have been in the business.

> *Mastery takes as long as you want it to take.*
> —*Tony Robbins*

And I'll say it again and again: you decide how fast you want to go and how good you want to get. You are in control of how you conduct your business, how you handle your paperwork, how you communicate with your clients, your fellow agents, whether or not you keep your deadlines, and everything in-between.

Build a world-class business that raises the bar in our industry, **and inspires others to aim higher as well.**

BRANDING STRATEGIES THAT WILL SET YOU APART

We're finally getting to *Stage 2* of the Market Domination Plan—your market presence. Assuming that you've already found <u>a brokerage that supports your mission and your goals,</u> let's talk about how to create a really sharp and super memorable brand, and how to craft a crystal-clear marketing message that communicates your distinct positioning within your marketplace.

1. A Memorable Brand

Even though your current brokerage will most likely have its own established brand and an adherence policy in place, there is still a lot you can do to take it to the next level. Instead of me trying to give you a five-step formula on how to do that, allow me to take you down memory lane, and share with you the story and evolution of *my* brand. I hope it inspires you and gets your creative juices flowing!

Since the very beginning of my career, people used to always ask me whether I am related to the race car driver, Michael Schumacher. #clue

Well, I am not, at least I don't think I am, even though we used to live only about forty kilometers from where Michael lived when we still lived back in Germany.

Whatever the case, it became obvious to me that I should probably make use of that in my brand because at the time, more times than not, it seemed to be a conversation starter. And so, even before I started my own company and had full control over what my brand would look and feel like, I started using the slogan:

"With Alina Schumacher, you're not just in the race—you WIN the race."

Kind of cool, says it all … although, to be honest, it still felt a bit wordy. No brand is going to be perfect from day one—it's something you will continue to work on and refine.

When I finally started my own company, **I was ready to engage the race theme on all twelve cylinders!** My colors were red, black, and white. I got one of those cool, red race suits and a helmet, we did a professional photo shoot and with the help of Photoshop, we also got some Ferraris into the picture—literally—which was brutally expensive back then. Photoshopping, that is. In fact, I remember having to pay my graphic designer between $500–$1,000 to get something as simple as a background removed from a picture so it's either transparent or just simply white. But I digressed.

Every single one of our marketing pieces—business cards, signage, stationary, feature sheets, CMA reports, website, postcards, etc.— had a super consistent layout with our unique logo components and always the same fonts and colors.

My slogan evolved to now simply being DRIVEN TO FINISH because the finish line is all about winning and helping my clients win was what I was passionate about.

When our properties sold, we *didn't* install a SOLD sign.

We installed a ***FINISHED*** sign, which between you and me, drove my competition nuts (pardon the pun) because even though they copied countless of my strategies over the years ... *THIS* one was impossible to copy.

People loved the brand and were super excited to have a ***FINISHED*** sign on their lawn. The colors and the checkers made people recognize our signs from far away. It was unmistakable, and ... it was awesome!!

By the way, can you sense my level of passion and excitement as you're reading this? That is exactly what I want for you. You've *GOT* to be excited about your brand. Otherwise, how are your clients supposed to be, right?

Go Big or Go Home!

When you are planning your business brand launch—or relaunch—you've got to be very strategic about it. You cannot tip-toe into the marketplace. And if you want to create the greatest amount of momentum and market buzz—**especially on a low budget**—there is no second chance to make a great first impression.

When you think about some of your favorite brands, what exactly is it that comes to mind? Whether you're thinking about Nike, Apple, Starbucks, or, you name it … I'm willing to bet that what we appreciate most about these brands—whether we realize it or not—is the consistency. In other words, we know exactly what to expect.

A Starbucks coffee looks and tastes the same, regardless of whether you buy it in Canada, the US, Mexico, or even El Salvador. I've had the Caramel Macchiato in all four countries and it really does look and taste the same.

Since we already know that the average consumer needs to see a certain ad or new brand quite a few times before they start to actually notice and recognize it because we're being bombarded with so many of them on a daily basis, let's make the most of every touchpoint and opportunity and **be super consistent,** using the same headshot, logos, colors, fonts, layouts, etc., on every marketing piece we put out there.

In other words, let's not have one picture on your website and a different one on your Facebook page and Instagram profile, while your office website is still displaying the one you submitted when you first started...

The same goes for the fonts and colors you use. How often do you see someone's business card at a property that looks different from the feature sheet or even the For-Sale sign on the front lawn, for that matter? They're using multiple different email addresses and phone numbers ... no wonder the market place is confused and isn't paying attention.

So, starting with the intangibles, what do you want your brand to look and feel like? Classy? Fun? Minimalistic? Bold? Luxurious?

Even the simplest things such as the colors, fonts, and the individual logo components will create a certain impression and perception, and with that, attract a certain type of prospect! Who are you trying to attract? What is the message you are wanting to convey?

Next, let's create a **consistent look and layout** for everything you publish—whether in print or online—and actually follow or enforce that with your suppliers.

Speaking of suppliers, now is also a good time to get a good understanding on all the different advertising vehicles available in your market area, including print media such as flyers, real estate magazines, the local community paper, the local real estate board paper, etc., and start getting info on pricing, ad size, design specifications, ad deadlines, as well as what the weekly/monthly distribution numbers are. **Yes, people still DO read the paper—** you just have to go about it the right way. More on that soon.

Try to also get an easy to remember phone number as well as a really easy to spell URL for your email and website address. If you can still get your name, great! However, instead of building your real estate website and brand around your name URL (which in most cases, is probably tricky to spell—unless it's Mary Brown), why not choose one that reflects the neighborhood or town you are wanting to establish in?

For example, SpringfieldAcreages.com—or in our case, we used our company slogan, DrivenToFinish.com—and then just forwarded any other domain names we had, including my personal name domain, to that one. By the way, notice above how much easier it is to read and remember when you capitalize each word in your domain name.

Next, let's get a website that doesn't just look pretty, **but actually has a purpose.** To do that, ask yourself: what do you want your buyer or seller prospects to think and believe about you when they visit your site? What do you want them to discover or learn? What do you want them to experience? And most importantly, <u>what do you want them to do</u> *before* they leave?

One of the <u>most profitable things I ever put on my homepage</u> was a little red box on the right sidebar that said:

BECOME A VIP Buyer And Get Priority Access
To My Upcoming Listings!

When a visitor clicked that little red box, it would take them to a simple page where they could type in their name, contact info, some search criteria for the property they were looking for, as well as the rough price range. The system would then send me an email with the info, and as you already know, instant follow up is key, and it is something you definitely want to become known for. In fact, people would always say, *"Holy! You are FAST!"* ... to which my reply was, *"Driven To Finish, Sir, how may I help you?"* —but I digressed.

My follow up process included a quick, personal email acknowledging what they signed up for (so there is congruency), then I'd explained the process of how I work and what to expect because everybody likes clarity. I would also give them my direct cell number, and schedule reminders to follow-up and keep in touch regularly.

Depending on the situation, I'd sometimes meet with them at the office and go over the process in person. Nothing complicated here, and yet over the years, **I've literally made hundreds of thousands of dollars in commissions with this simple strategy** because people came to our site, loved how cool and different it was, connected with the clear message ... and *priority access* is a no-brainer—especially once you're starting to gain some traction in the marketplace.

YOUR SIGNAGE

Next, let's get your signage ready or updated, and let's make sure you invest in a decent quality, UV coated product. Nothing worse than a *red* that slowly turns into *pink.* **Your signage is hands down your very best lead generator and offline social proof.**

In fact, my team surveyed all my incoming calls for about three years, and when we asked people how they found out about us, they'd consistently say:

"Oh. I see her signs everywhere!!"

You may not have any listings yet, but you will very soon. And when you do, let's make the most of it!

MY FIRST LISTING SIGNAGE '*STRATEGY*'

I still have to chuckle when I think about **the very first listing I ever got.** It was a fixer-upper situated on a lovely acreage along a small creek that was notorious for flooding! And every single spring, this quaint little place would only be accessible via a canoe.

I had 47 *showings* on that place within a two-week time-frame until I finally found a buyer who was adventurous (and athletic?) enough to changing up their means of transportation to the house every now and then—every spring, to be exact. Probably an *Enneagram 7*.

Thankfully, I had it listed in the fall.

Otherwise, who knows … with 47 showings … **I might have gotten seasick or something!** Just kidding.

To make my point, though, since I was so excited to finally have a listing, I literally installed a directional sign from every direction you could have possibly come from—including the detours.

My broker at the time was merciless in making fun of me, wondering why I didn't just connect all those signs with a red ribbon!?

But guess what? It worked and it definitely had the exact effect I was shooting for because, even the people in my church came up to me on Sunday mornings, wondering how things were going, and "that I must be doing really well because they see my signs everywhere". Boom!

The bottom line is, as someone very wise once said: "If you fail to plan, you're planning to fail."

Most agents do a little bit of this and a little bit of that ... and end up with a whole lot of expenses and <u>nothing to show for it.</u>

Let's be more strategic in our planning and execution of things. And when you're ready to launch, let's turn a few heads and give the impression of ... *"Who is that gal? I see her face everywhere!"*

Consistency is key.

2. A Clear Marketing Message and Distinct Positioning

Now, let's create a unique marketing message that clearly conveys what you do, who you serve specifically and where, and the unique benefit or result your clients can expect by working with *you* versus the other 5,000 agents in town. In other words, imagine if someone asked you what you do—your response to that question is what I'm talking about ... <u>but not like most agents would answer it.</u>

My coaching clients know this as *the one-liner.*

<u>For example:</u>

I help homeowners in the Springfield area sell their homes faster and for <u>MORE</u> money using my <u>proprietary "Ready, Set, Go Strategy"</u> that takes out the guesswork and stress from the home selling experience, and helps them get to their new place <u>FASTER!</u>

When you go to my website, www.AlinaSchumacher.com, you will see that one-liner in action in my capacity as a coach. There is a short version right on the top banner, as well as the full version in the welcome message.

Your website should have the same thing.

My son, who has been doing our real estate photography since he was 15, recently started his own real estate photography business, and his one-liner is:

I help Winnipeg agents stand out from the competition by providing them with scroll-stopping Real Estate Videography and Photography that helps them sell their listings faster, for more money, and create happy clients!

Here's what this does:

Besides clearly stating what you do, **it helps people to self-qualify or self-disqualify themselves from potentially working with you.**

See, I dominated the Springfield area—more specifically, my specialty was upscale acreages close to a very desirable provincial park that heavily influenced property values. That's what I became known for.

If you happened to see my marketing and you were NOT from Springfield and had NO intentions of moving there, you'd just keep scrolling … or turning the pages. If you were interested in buying or selling there, however, or knew someone who is, my marketing message would grab your attention.

And you might be thinking, *"But, Alina, isn't that limiting my options? Wouldn't I be leaving a lot of cash on the table that way?"*

It depends on how you think about marketing and what you want to be known for. In my case, if people were looking for an agent in general, they had lots of options. But, if they wanted to buy close to Birds Hill Park, people would say, *"You have to call Alina, she's the queen of Springfield, and she has all the best listings there."* (However cliché that may sound, it worked.)

Besides, specializing in a specific geographical area doesn't mean that you never list or sell anything outside of that area. When people came to my Open Houses because they were interested in *moving* to Springfield, and eventually bought a place, they would almost always ask me to also sell their *existing* home in *xyz* town or neighborhood.

And, of course, there will be plenty of local people whose homes you're going to sell who are going to be moving outside of your area of expertise. And if you have a great working relationship, and it is feasible, you're obviously going to help them with that as well.

It's the **quality versus quantity** approach, and instead of focusing on the limitations that such distinct positioning could potentially pose, think of the *quality of clients* you are going to be attracting.

The bottom line is:

When you need brain surgery, you don't go to a general doctor—you go to the SPECIALIST. And we all know that a specialist is more expensive and more in demand ... because they have a higher and more specialized level of training, skill, and experience. What's that worth?

To summarize: Let's create a consistent brand experience as well as a clear marketing message and **distinct positioning that is magnetic to your ideal audience** and in your specific niche, while tastefully repelling the not so ideal audience.

It's time to get more tactical. Are you ready?

HOW TO BUILD MASSIVE MOMENTUM & GOODWILL, FAST!

Now that you have thoroughly done the preparation work and feel super confident, and have a unique brand as well as all the tangible marketing components in place, let's talk about the *intangible* parts of your brand which essentially is what people are saying about you—or in other words—**market buzz!**

When people talk about you, your business, and your values, what do you want them to say? What do you want to be known for—other than that you're ... **a Ree-luh-tor?**

> *You can get everything in life you want if you will just help enough other people get what they want.*
> —Zig Ziglar

From very early on in my career, there was this one thing that I was extremely passionate about, and that is to help people who cannot help themselves. Remember my childhood dream that I shared with you earlier?

If you think about it, we are in the business of helping people find their next perfect home. But how many people are out there, living on the streets, who've never really experienced what it's like to have a loving, comfortable, warm, and accepting home?

I used to drive down the streets downtown, thinking, *"Why don't you guys just get a job and get your life together ... and go to work like everyone else does?"* It seems like a valid question, and even though I regularly gave money to the homeless shelters in our town, I still would sometimes feel a level of reluctance.

I mean, I had to work for it too, right?

It wasn't until I started to research the topic, tour the facilities, and have conversations with real people who *have been there*, and who were able to make the transition back to what we would call 'normal life', that I started to understand what really causes and sometimes forces people to live on the street. And the way the system works, it is nearly impossible for them to ever get back on their feet...

My heart was forever changed.

Imagine the wife who has no one. No friends, no family. She gets beat up by her intoxicated husband every single night until one night, she runs away, just to end up in even worse circumstances. True story ...

Imagine the foster child, who has already lived in 32 different homes, and still gets moved around again and again. He keeps running away because he can't handle the pain of being unwanted, but imagine what living on the streets will look like. Abuse, and more abuse—unless you become the abuser. True story …

Imagine a middle-aged man, whose wife has cancer. Bills are piling up, and he loses his job because the pain and the suffering of his wife—and all the sleepless nights—caused him to stay away from work more than he should have. He was like the average North American, who's debt load caused him to be only one and half months away from bankruptcy.

When he lost his house, he also lost his address. **Without an address, you cannot maintain a social security number.** Without a social security number, you cannot get a legal job. Without a job, you cannot pay for a place to live—a.k.a. the address. It's a vicious cycle. And where I live, it's really cold in the winter … and this stuff really happens.

And I could go on and on.

I knew I needed to do more than just give money. I needed to start raising awareness somehow and educate people on the real reasons of homelessness—*AND* how our often ignorant, 'conscience-satisfying', year-end, tax-deductible charity efforts actually make things worse. Because if all we do is feed those people and give them handouts, **we take away their dignity and reinforce their dependency.** Worse yet … we take away their hope of ever being able to break that cycle. The homeless shelter in my town understood that, and, as a result, had incredible rehab programs that *REALLY* helped people. Once I grasped the power of that and saw people's lives actually restored, I was on fire.

Now, what does *any* of this have to do with real estate or MARKETING???

Keep reading with an open mind, and I promise you will catch this.

So, what could I do to raise awareness? My beginnings were humble, and since the shelter desperately needed cash due to a huge leadership fiasco they had just gone through which caused a few really big donors to pull out, I figured I would organize a fundraiser that would not only raise money, but also educate people and help them understand the real issues of homelessness and how the 'system' really works.

So, that particular year, I had this crazy idea of doing a bake sale where I was going to match dollar for dollar what we would sell in baked goods and receive in donations.

My marketing campaign included me in my red race suit, the shot showed me taking off the helmet, and the headline was something like: *"Join me in raising $10,000 Dollars for XYZ Mission as I* *trade my Helmet for a Baker's Hat,"* along with our *Driven To Finish* brand all over it, of course.

Now, when you do something like this, your goal is obviously not to toot your own horn and do a charitable deed so you can be seen. However, if your heart is in the right place and you truly *DO* want to make a difference, watch what can happen…

To get the word out, we got sponsorships from various local papers who either gave us ad space at a ridiculously reduced rate or completely for free in return for recognition. We also lined up some interviews on the local radio stations that helped us spread the word. We got a whole bunch of excited volunteers who became our *walking billboards* and brought even more publicity and traffic.

Long story short, when the big day finally arrived, we sold out within three hours, **and our story landed on the front cover** of the local community newspaper.

And I know you're probably picturing this quaint little farmers market, people laughing and having fun, carrying their organic produce while sipping their locally roasted coffee … running into people they haven't seen in a while.

That's what I had planned.

However, **it ended up raining the entire time we were there**—which we weren't prepared for—and which made the community's support even more incredible!

It was a humble start, but we ended up raising over $13,000 that day, selling nothing but cinnamon buns, cheesecakes, European-style tortes (I used to make wedding cakes for friends back in Germany), and some good ol' fashioned pies. And don't forget, this was before social media. Imagine the incredible reach we could have had with that!

And you might be thinking, *What's 13 grand gonna do...? That's a drop in a bucket!*

I agree.

It doesn't even come close to covering even one month of that mission's payroll. But **change starts with changing our beliefs.**

Imagine the cumulative effect if your influence and example was able to change even one single human being's beliefs and open their heart and soul? And imagine if, instead of just being more *NOISE* in the marketplace, promoting your*SELF,* and trying to convince people that you're the best agent in town—you did something entirely different and truly meaningful—while positioning your business in such a way that in the mind of the people who live in your market area, there *is* no competition for you?

Because you created a wonderful and <u>very memorable</u> event for your community; you advocated and united them for a worthy cause, and best of all, **you were never the center of attention,** even though your name was all over it.

The side effect? Your business got a ton of free exposure *WHILE* you were drawing the attention to *helping each other and raising the community spirit.* People will be talking about that for years to come.

Marketing, after all, is ... a conversation. What <u>you</u> give is a lot of love, care, compassion, hard work ... and 100% integrity behind everything you do.

Quick Time Out: Fundraisers aren't new. The shift that will make all the difference, however, is when you turn an event into a movement. For that to happen, you have to *be* the spotlight—instead of being *in* the spotlight.

THE CIRCLE OF LOVE GALA

After that experience, I started to rack my brain about how in the world I could scale this ... because let's face it, it was a *LOT* of work. So, this one night, as I was watching an Amy Grant concert while folding laundry that was spread out all over my king-sized bed, I had this crazy idea ...

What if I hosted a concert? What if I stepped out of my comfort zone and sang to raise money … would people actually show up?

It was the middle of November, and I instantly called a meeting with two very special friends who had a ton of experience hosting events (golf tournaments, including *The Players Cup*) and the social clout to make this happen. Truth is, I could have never pulled this off without them, especially not the date I had in mind, and their connections and immense support truly made it possible.

I also happened to know one of the most talented musical prodigies in the province, who headed up the band for me, and just three months later, **on Valentine's Day,** my crazy idea became a sparkling reality.

The Circle of Love Gala, hosted at one of the finest venues in our city, became our annual event, and it truly was a glamorous and very exclusive experience. It was targeted specifically towards business owners (think sponsorships and networking), and our guests got to enjoy a beautiful four-course dinner, fun entertainment, and a chance to win some very awesome prizes, incl. all-inclusive trips to the Caribbean, golf memberships, staging packages, and much more.

Most importantly, however, they got to experience a virtual tour of the mission's shelter and hear the heart-warming, transformational stories of real people who were able to escape that lifestyle with *the right* kind of help. It doesn't get much more inspiring than to see that your dollars really can make such an impact on a human being's life.

The really great part of an event like this is the opportunity to *leverage your reach*. You can invite popular public figures and business owners to emcee and join you on the planning committee. You can even invite local political representatives to bring greetings from their respective parties—which, in turn, will open the doors to more great connections and maximize your sponsorships and prize donation options. Don't forget about those lawyer, builder, and mortgage broker friends you made! Every business owner loves a networking opportunity as well as their name in the event program!

The Benefits of an Event Like This Truly are *UNQUANTIFIABLE*

It adds so much value to the charity. Because not only do they get the proceeds from the event and all that great exposure, but they're also getting new supporters who were able to change their mind about the situation because they had an opportunity to hear and see firsthand what it's really like.

And compassion enriches anyone's life!

It also adds value to your guests. Undoubtedly, they made some new friends, struck up some new business deals ... and perhaps even won a trip to the Caribbean!

What about the volunteers who joined you in the effort? My team and I learned so much when we were doing these events because we all got to participate in something that was so much bigger than ourselves, and that <u>truly enriched our team culture.</u>

And finally, it benefits your business like hardly anything else ever could. As the spokesperson and advocate, you get a ton of free publicity and brand exposure through various kinds of media, such as interviews and support from your local radio and TV stations, articles and ads in local print media, and of course ... social media exposure.

Your vision for the event is on every marketing piece, and you get to exclusively set yourself apart <u>not based on who you say you are</u> but based on what you're passionate about, **and what you're willing to do about it!**

And when people see your ads and for sale signs out there, their perception of you is entirely different than of a typical real estate agent. They may have never been to any of your events yet, but they have seen your marketing and advocating for the common good, they have heard good things about you ... and those are the seeds of trust.

Obviously, I'm not saying that you should go and advocate for the homeless. You may want to do something entirely different!

There are so many worthy causes. Pick something that you and your community are passionate about, and remember to <u>always be the spotlight, shining the light on others</u>—instead of having it shine on you.

If you do this right and with the right heart attitude ... your business is going to explode. Get ready!

COMMUNITY CONTESTS

Community contests and challenges, especially seasonal, are another simple, but really great way to uniquely engage the people in your marketplace, and social media is perfect to announce and market those. Plus, it's free! Here are three examples that I've personally used with great success. I'm sure they will get your creative juices flowing and help you to come up with many more ideas that are relevant to your specific audience and market area.

1. Christmas Coloring Contest for Kids

This campaign is especially great if your target audience is younger families with kids, and for this contest, we simply posted a photo of our undecorated office Christmas tree along with an ornament image and asked the kids in our community to help us decorate it!

All they had to do was to print and cut out the ornament, decorate it to their heart's content #glitteroverload and then either mail it in or drop it off at our office. Obviously, the parents played a big part in this since they were the ones who would've seen the post on social or in the local community paper, encouraged their kids to participate, and then helped them with the project and the delivery part.

A contest like that is so simple to pull off, and as the submissions keep coming in, you can post photos of each masterpiece on your social media platforms—a.k.a. original content that's relevant—and that people love to see. You can mention the kids' first names in the caption of each post, and encourage other kids to participate as well. Don't forget to create a custom hashtag, like #SpringfieldKidsColoringContest. Notice, there's nothing in there about my name or company.

Once again, **being *the* spotlight versus being *in* the spotlight.**

The cool thing is that Moms and Dads will be happy and proud to like and share your post of their kid's ornament submission, which gives you awesome exposure and social proof.

Make sure to disclose all the contest rules upfront, including how old the kids have to be to qualify, as well as the date and exact time of the draw, and then do the draw LIVE on Facebook to build even more buzz and momentum!

Your prizes could be gift cards to a toy store or local specialty shoppe, and can easily be sponsored in return for generous shoutouts and recognition. When the winners come to your office to pick up their prize, ask for permission to snap a photo together and post it to your Facebook page.

And finally, don't forget to thank everyone for their beautiful work and submissions, and invite them to participate again next year!

I realize most agents will probably <u>write this off as fluff and a waste of time</u> ... and that's cool. I mean, imagine if every single agent in your area was running a kid's coloring contest—**it would be a gong show!**

Just make sure *you* don't write it off, and instead of wasting money on glossy self-promo ads, telling people how awesome you are, let *THEM* talk about you.

Works a lot better.

2. Golf Tourney

Golf tournaments are very common, regardless of where you live, and this contest here is super easy to host. I have title-sponsored a local charity golf tournament for many years, and while we always tried to do something fun and unique for the players at our sponsor hole, this one year we did a dress up contest that turned out to be the talk of the event.

We got boxes full of funny wigs, hats, glasses, and other funny accessories, and each foursome was presented with the challenge to dress up, use our props, and pose for the funniest group photo!

We then quickly branded each photo with a custom event banner and posted them to our Facebook page. Each group was encouraged to share the post with their group photo to their own Facebook profiles along with the custom hashtag we created, and the group that would get the most comments, likes, and shares at the end of the event would win a gift card for an all-inclusive dinner for eight people—sponsored, of course—and the draw took place during dinner in the clubhouse.

We received a huge amount of exposure and engagement with this campaign, not to mention all the great conversations with the 150+ players during the event! It was definitely the highlight of that tourney, and people kept talking about it **long after the free margaritas and soggy chicken wings** from the other sponsors were forgotten. (Don't tell them I said that!)

3. The Awesome Neighbor Contest

This was probably the coolest contest idea I've ever had, if I do say so myself. It literally came to me as I was looking through some video footage on my phone. Specifically, some shots I had taken of an old house being torn down on one of our investment properties. I know … my brain works in strange ways sometimes.

Anyways, this contest was all about encouraging people to pause and reflect on what matters most in our lives, and that is relationships—in this case, our relationships with our neighbors. And I know we all have that one oddball on our street, but we also have amazing neighbors that go over and above. And this contest was encouraging people to recognize and nominate that neighbor and share a story where they did something remarkably special for someone else in the neighborhood without being in the spotlight.

We shot a cool contest promo video—this is where that old house demolition video footage comes in, by the way, and I strategically involved some of the community's most influential citizens, which got us a ton of extra exposure. In the end, even the local community newspaper caught the buzz and did a great article. We got a number of truly remarkable story submissions—some of them literally made me cry.

There is so much goodness and kindness all around us if we just take the time to pause and notice, and <u>my goal with this campaign was to acknowledge those special people in our lives,</u> *and shine that spotlight on them.*

Be the change you want to see in this world.

—Gandhi

I hope this chapter inspired you <u>to think even bigger</u> and realize all the amazing opportunities we have to serve and add value to people, go the extra mile, and with that, create a solid reputation that precedes us.

It's time to shift gears. You ready?

SKILL 7

MARKETING & TRAFFIC SECRETS FROM THE FAST LANE

What comes to mind when you hear the word *marketing*? To most agents, marketing just means advertising and **getting their name out there**.

So, they ...

- Pin their business card on every local gas station pin board in town—next to the other 57 agents.
- Run expensive self-promo ads in glossy magazines and local newspapers, promising to "guide you home" while they are "outstanding in their field".
- Door-knock and leave *door hangers* and goldfish on people's doors with the note, "fishing for referrals".
- Sneak their business card in the candy they hand out to kids on Halloween.
- Send out those pesky letters in the mail that promise "a buyer for your home".
- Etc.

I bet you could add a dozen more to this list. It's pretty safe to say that **agents do not lack creativity** when it comes to trying to get their market's attention.

Be honest though, if you ACTUALLY had to buy or sell a house and you didn't know any agent in town—would you call the guy whose card you found in your kid's Halloween candy pile??? Or the one who's card was pinned on your local gas station pin board? What would you do with the door hanger ... or the goldfish?

All of that is called _chasing._

What if we turned that around, and instead of chasing, we started to attract by becoming irresistibly magnetic to our ideal prospects—in other words, the people that fit a certain, predetermined criteria, and that you would actually like to work with?

To get started, let's get clear on the following five questions:

1. Who is your ideal target audience? Who do you really want to work with? What are their demographics and characteristics?
2. What do those people want? What are their dreams, aspirations, and changing lifestyle wants and needs?
3. What challenges or obstacles are in the way of getting what they want? What problems are they trying to solve?

4. What are they worried about or afraid of?
5. What questions do they need answered in order to move forward?

With those five questions answered, I believe that <u>marketing is</u> any and all activity that is intended to get the attention of your ideal target audience, inviting them on a journey of discovery, awareness, and education—while pre-framing their perception of you, building trust and confidence, and showing them exactly how you can help them get from where they are to where they want to be with the least amount of detours and damage—a.k.a. the *Invitation.*

Who are you trying to reach, and what do those people <u>really</u> want?

If your target audience is younger families, for example, they might be dreaming of living in a better and safer neighborhood. They might need more space for their growing family—perhaps an attached garage—because they're tired of hauling in the groceries and baby car seats in the rain, and having to scrape their icy windshield every morning in the winter.

If you're specializing in working with people who are closer to retirement age, they're probably looking for a lifestyle with less work and the freedom to travel whenever they want. In other words, no more lawnmowers and snowblowers in their lives! Perhaps also a few less stairs and a little quieter neighbors?

If you're specializing in a specific geographical area, development, or community, like I used to, for example, the perks of living there might be bigger lots, lower taxes, safer communities where kids still play outside, being close to city limits—and yet away from all the hustle and bustle of city living, right?

The best kind of marketing is entering a conversation your prospects are already having in their mind, because it goes under the radar and isn't perceived as marketing, per se. That conversation is never about products or services.

Nobody has ever woken up in the middle of the night, and exclaimed out loud, *"Martha! I got it! A proven marketing plan and cutting-edge marketing tools is what we need to sell this place!"*

That's technobabble ... and your marketplace doesn't think and talk that way! Their conversations are about their changing lifestyle needs, and the resulting dreams and aspirations that promise to improve their quality of life. (Or ... adjust it, in some cases.)

And if you understand your ideal prospect's dreams and aspirations, as well as their fears, worries, and challenges, **and you're able to describe them better than *they can do themselves* in your marketing content—you will get their attention.**

Think about the last time you thought about selling your existing home and buying one that would better accommodate your changing lifestyle needs. If you're like most people and don't have unlimited cash resources, there's undoubtedly going to be an internal battle. On one hand, there is <u>that new quality of life you're daydreaming about,</u> and all the wonderful things that would make life so much better <u>if only</u> ... fill in the blanks.

On the other hand, however, there are all these fears. The fear of the unknown, the fear of the potential risk involved, the fear of making a mistake or the wrong decision, the fear of missing *the* dream home **because the old one isn't selling as quickly as expected,** the fear of ending up with two houses or two mortgages ... and an even bigger financial burden.

Guess what? Your prospects are exactly the same!

And that is WHY 99% of the "marketing" that most agents spent their money on is completely useless!

People won't work with you because they got your notepad in the mail or saw your face on a bus bench or their grocery shopping cart. **They don't care about you!** (As much as you don't care about me, but about whether or not I can actually help you.)

People don't care about how awesome <u>you say</u> you are, how many awards you've got, how fancy your listing presentation is or how *cutting-edge* your marketing tools are.

What they care about is ... themselves—as harsh as this may sound. And with the internal battle going on, their focus is on trying to figure out <u>how they can get from where they are to where they want to be</u> with the least amount of risk and without jeopardizing the safety and comfort of their family.

Your service is just <u>the vehicle that gets them to their desired destination.</u> So instead of sitting there, parked on the side of the road, and trying to sell the *vehicle,* telling everyone how fast and how awesome it is—be **the bus that's already moving *TOWARDS* your ideal audience's destination!**

How?

The strategy that I'm about to share with you on the next few pages is going to show you how and will get you results faster than you can imagine. It's simple, friendly, and really helpful to people. Best of all, **99% of all agents will never do it,** so if you're NOT like 99% of all agents, you're golden.

Just follow the formula, and <u>you can be the local trusted authority on all things real estate in as little as a month or two.</u>

Don't believe me? There's only one way to find out. My job is to teach you—yours is to do the work <u>and get paid.</u>

Deal?

THE TWO-STEP FACEBOOK CLIENT ATTRACTION MODEL THAT'S WORKING NOW

So, what's the strategy? It's a two-step process that starts with creating strategic content that is magnetic to your ideal target audience via Facebook LIVE broadcasts and then running ads to the people that actually engage with that content.

In other words: Instead of sharing cat videos and other *irrelevant* fluff with the Facebook world, **let's post content that ANSWERS the questions your ideal target audience is already asking** as a result of that internal battle we just discussed, and with that, start moving them from where they are, to where they want to be.

A confused mind never buys, however, <u>if you are able to help them get clarity</u> on the things they're trying to figure out, even before they voice them, you automatically move up on their value and trust ladder.

That sentence right there is worth studying.

OK, I Get It, But ... LIVE? Are You Serious?

I realize this takes any normal human being way outside of their comfort zone ... until you've done it a few times.

So, let's go back to the foundation: Why did you want to dominate your market again? What was the *Big Why* you were willing to fight for, regardless of what life throws at you?

"Ya, but ... couldn't I just make a few videos of me answering those questions, cut together the best takes ... and post that? That would look so much more professional than ... doing it LIVE!"

Not for the effect we are shooting for right now. First of all, raw and real is what connects most in today's market because people are tired of filtered and edited. And that is not to say that you shouldn't practice your presentation skills, but people connect with human, not with perfect.

Plus, once again, they don't really care about you, remember? They care about what you can do for them because their focus is on the problem they're trying to solve.

Secondly, there's the algorithm. Nobody really understands it, but numbers don't lie. LIVE broadcasts have a far greater reach than uploaded videos. In fact, some say as far as ten times the reach!

So, **if you want to keep going on the fast lane** and are planning to win, you must be willing to do what most people will never do, so that very soon, you can have what most people will never have - still my favorite quote by Thomas Jefferson.

So, what are you going to talk about in your LIVE Broadcasts?

If you completed the previous exercise and answered those five questions, this next step is easy. If you haven't yet, let's go back and do that first.

Essentially, the ANSWERS to the questions that <u>your</u> ideal prospects in <u>your</u> target niche and location are asking is the content that you're going to be talking about in your LIVE broadcasts.

<u>Don't worry, I'll give you the exact framework in a second.</u>

Here are a few examples:

"I don't know where to start. What's the process? What should I do first? Do I interview multiple agents?"

"What do I have to do to get my house ready for the market?"

"Should I replace the shingles before I list?"

"Is it better to list in the spring?"

"What if it doesn't sell right away?"

"What if my neighbors show up at the open house?"

"Should I repaint the kids' bedrooms before I list? They are orange, green, and pink!"

"They always say: Depersonalize! Should I take down <u>all</u> my family pictures?"

"What about my pets? What do I do with them during showings when I'm at work?"

"What happens if our house doesn't sell before we have to move? Do vacant homes sell for *less* money?"

"Do I buy first and then sell? Or, do I sell first?"

"Should I even bother listing with an agent? The market is hot, couldn't I just sell it myself and save the commission?"

… I could go on and on. The examples I just gave are more generic to give you a head start, and you can obviously make them a lot more relevant to your specific audience.

Quick Timeout: You might be thinking that all that information is common sense and everybody knows that, but **the insight that you are taking for granted** is the connecting piece that will help you to build trust with your marketplace.

How about this question here: ***"How do I choose the best agent for me?"*** How would you answer that question intelligently, objectively, and yet ... strategically?

Here's the **framework** that I promised, and then I'll give you a word-for-word example:

1. Start with your one-liner
2. Tell people what the video will be about (intriguing title)
3. Include a story or an analogy
4. Offer valuable insight and advice (the answer to the question your video is about)
5. Include a non-salesy CTA, summarizing your one-liner (Call To Action)

Like so:

"Hey, this is Alina Schumacher, coming to you LIVE from the Headquarters of Schumacher Realty, and I help homeowners in the Springfield area sell their homes faster, and for MORE money using my proven and 'proprietary' Ready, Set, Go Winning Strategy that takes out the guesswork, worries, and the stress from the home selling experience and helps them get to their new place FASTER!

And the question that I hear people ask quite often, especially when they start their home-selling journey is, "How do I choose the best Realtor for me?"

Have you ever wondered about that? It's such a great question, because there are so many options, and so many different approaches out there, right?

Like, do you hire the Realtor that charges the least commission or the one that has the most signs in town? What if the agent is new? How do you know who's REALLY the best choice for you—specifically?

And this reminds me of an experience I had just a few months ago, and tell me if you've ever been in this situation, but ... we were getting one of our investment properties ready for the market, and we kind of last-minute decided that we should probably give it a fresh coat of paint!

And I had this thought of doing it myself because I actually enjoy it, in fact, I even started buying paint and rollers, but then, you know, life gets in the way, and we decided that we should probably leave it to the professionals.

So, I called multiple painters. A few of them never returned my call, but thankfully, a couple of them did show up to give me a quote. One of them made it sound like this was quite the job, and he kept pointing out all kinds of deficiencies, and overall, just made us feel like he was doing us a huge favor! He was saying over and over again how busy he was, and that he would have to send one of his crews after hours to do it in stages.

The other guy showed up, and I kid you not, he had a bounce in his step, and he kept paying us compliments on the property, the kitchen—he totally loved the island—and he was constantly saying: "Beautiful!" His enthusiasm was literally contagious! He was also busy, but he assured us that he can make it work and that he understood our deadline and urgency of wanting to get the property on the market as soon as possible!

Tell me, judging by these facts (because at this point, we don't even know how much, right?) ... would you pick the painter that was cheaper, or the one that had the great attitude? In this case, I'm happy to say that the guy with the great attitude came in a little bit cheaper than the other guy, but to be honest, if it had been the other way around, I would have still hired him.

And so, when you're ready to hire a Realtor who's gonna be representing you in selling your home, which is such a major event in anybody's life, right? And it's not always about who's gonna give you the best deal on the commission! There's something to be said about a great attitude and an awesome work ethic!

*Besides ... **a lower percentage doesn't necessarily translate into a higher net profit,** because if you do the math ... 5% of 300K still leaves you with more in your pockets than 3% of 290K! Right?*

So how do you choose the best agent for you?

Here's what I would suggest—and obviously, as you know, I'm doing this for a living—but my goal is to give you an objective opinion and help you make the best decision for you.

I would interview at least two or three agents, and I'd look at their actual results, their market knowledge, their professionalism, their ability to listen well and ask great questions, and of course ... their attitude. And then, when you find the one who you feel most confident in, then discuss commission. And I think you will find this to be the best and most profitable way of doing business!

Hey, thanks so much for tuning in! Again, I am Alina Schumacher with Schumacher Realty, and I so, so appreciate you taking the time to watch this video! I hope you found this information helpful. If you have any questions whatsoever, or are thinking about making a move in the future, feel free to call me at 444-3000—I know the race track really well, and I'll take you to the finish line!"

Just like that.

And next time they see another one of your videos on social, they will be even more open and receptive to what you have to say because it's helpful, it's interesting ... and just different. They might even share it with a friend who's thinking of buying or selling as well!

The bottom line of this strategy is to demonstrate to your marketplace that you can help them ... by actually helping them, and with that, intentionally build trust and goodwill with your ideal prospects **before they are getting ready to buy or sell.**

And when they are, you're already the top of mind expert because you added so much value to them and really helped them.

Quick Time Out: You might be thinking, "But Alina ... didn't you say you're going to teach me the exact strategies you used to build your business? There was no Facebook LIVE back in 2005!"

You're right. There was no Facebook LIVE when I started my business. In fact, there wasn't even a Facebook yet, per se, even though it apparently launched in 2004, according to Google. My first ever official FB Business Page post was on October 14, 2010.

Unimaginable how much faster I could have accelerated my business growth had I had the tools and marketing insight that you are having right now. Imagine *your* possibilities!!

The very first LIVE Facebook broadcast I ever did was back at the end of 2015, which is when it became available to small businesses. And the best way I knew to use it back then was to simply give people preview tours of my upcoming property listings, showing my team *on set*, doing photos, video, flying the drone, installing signage, etc. In other words, building anticipation and excitement!

I did use the strategy I'm teaching you in this chapter via blog posts though, which, obviously was nowhere near as fast and effective as video because, for one, people much rather watch something than read, secondly, written words are easy to copy, which makes it more difficult to really stand out.

We had a few different domains based on the type of audience I was trying to reach, including:

HomeSellingInsiderTips.com
SpringfieldHomeSalesReport.com
HomeBuyingInsiderTips.com

I strategically drove traffic to those domains—even though they all pointed to the same real estate blog—because it helped me to measure the ROI. And <u>those blog posts were all about answering the kinds of questions</u> that my ideal audience was wondering about.

To get back to the Facebook LIVE Content ...

As you continue to do more and more of these educational LIVE broadcasts, answering people's questions and sharing insight versus just information, you're not only building and nurturing an audience; <u>you're also growing your reach and engagement.</u>

The way the algorithm works is the more Facebook LIVE broadcasts you do, the more it will organically show your content in people's newsfeeds. Plus, chances are that there are a lot more people in your target market area than are currently following your Facebook page.

Once you have a few really good content pieces in place, you can start running ads to them, which grows your Facebook following and expands your reach even more. You'd be surprised how effective a $5-10 daily budget in Facebook ads can be.

Next, and this is crucial, Facebook has this awesome tool that allows you to create custom audiences of people who've specifically watched a certain percentage of your videos within a specific amount of days. (You can determine that.)

It takes about 30 seconds to create those in the Custom Audience area of the Business Manager on Facebook, and we can create multiple different Custom Audience variations for different purposes.

For example, one of those Custom Audiences could be all the people that watch at least 50% of your videos within the last 30 days.

As you continue to create engaging content with your LIVE videos regularly, the Facebook algorithm does its tracking magic and constantly updates that audience. In other words, it grows anytime someone watches at least 50% of any of your videos.

And this now allows you to create and run specific ads <u>only</u> to the people that are actually interested in your content and might be a potential future prospect/client.

If Your Eyes Are Glazing Over Right Now, and I'm Losing You, Just Think Back to the Good Ol' Days of ... Calculus.

Let's keep going!

Once we have built up some data, we move on to <u>Step Two</u> in this process, and we start creating strategic **ad campaigns** in the Facebook Business Manager, and have Facebook only show those ads to the accumulated, now *warm audience.*

RETARGETING ON FACEBOOK

You know how you sometimes <u>look for something specific on Amazon,</u> and then an ad with that same 'thing' starts following you around everywhere you go on the web? That is called retargeting. And yes, there is a way of doing it in a less aggressive and annoying manner.

First, you're going to need to create your Facebook Pixel in the Business Manager, install it on your website, and then ensure that it fires properly. The Google Chrome Pixel Helper extension is great for that.

The Facebook Pixel is a small piece of Java code that you (or whoever manages your website) copy and paste into the header code of your website. It literally takes ten seconds to do.

Even though it may sound complicated, it really isn't.

The purpose of the Pixel on your website is to track all of your website's traffic, which allows us to create another Custom Audiences within the Facebook Business Manager—specifically, all the people who have visited your site. In fact, you can segment those visitors into *buckets* of people who visited your site within the last 3, 7, 15, or 30 days—based on the advertising strategy you want to execute.

Once we have built up some data, we can start running direct response ads to those people specifically—**which is called retargeting.**

<u>Little insider tip</u> here: you may want to create a custom audience of all real estate agents in your city, so that you can easily exclude them from your ads—which means that they won't be seeing them in their newsfeed. #ninja

Your Facebook ads could be offering a report, such as:

- *"What are Homes in Springfield Selling For? Download a FREE 2020 Market Report Here!"*

- *"Thinking of Selling Your Home? Here's a report of Springfield Acreage Sales Prices for 2020. Instant FREE download."*

And remember, the people seeing these ads already know who you are because they have watched your videos!

You may also choose to run short-term ad campaigns like:

- An Open House invitation with, perhaps, a give-away alert
- New or upcoming listing ads
- Just SOLD campaigns with a client testimonial *(which is far more effective than the postcard version)*
- Community or charity events that you host or sponsor, etc.

Whatever you choose it to be—all these types of ads would only be targeted towards the people who have *already* shown an interest in your service.

If you want to go <u>even more ninja,</u> next time you have an Open House, run a Facebook ad campaign that *geofences* everyone in a specific location and run a special offer—with the proper disclaimers in place of course—as you don't want to be soliciting other agents' clients that are already under contract.

The way this works is, anyone who has their location services enabled on their phone and is in the specific geographical area that you *fenced in* within the Facebook ad targeting criteria will see your Open House ad along with your special offer on their phone.

Since they will only see your ad if they're actually in that location, chances are they are going to take action and visit your Open House!

The special offer could be something like:

"Looking to Buy in Springfield? Join me at my Open House at 123 Main this Sunday between 2-5 pm and enter our draw for an ALL-INCLUSIVE Housewarming Party For 20!"

Add the proper disclaimers of course, and get it sponsored ... but HELLOOOO?? Is this cool, or is this cool?

The **big mistake** 99% of agents (or their advertising agencies) are making with Facebook ads is they skip Step One—which is the expert-positioning, trust-building, and prospect-qualifying step, and move directly to Step Two.

And instead of only spending their advertising dollars on ads that are targeted towards the people who have already expressed an interest in their content, they run ads to everyone in town—in other words, completely cold audiences—**which is expensive and nowhere near as effective** as the strategy I just shared with you.

Once you have been doing Step One of this strategy for a while, however, and are starting to get some traction and name recognition in your marketplace, it's super easy to expand your reach into more colder audiences, and with that, get even more results.

As I mentioned in an earlier chapter, <u>you cannot tip-toe into the market.</u> You have to come in with confidence, power, a clear differentiation, and an unshakable desire to succeed. That requires strategic planning and preparation. Your focus should be on building **massive goodwill** and trust within your community. With that kind of foundation, you don't need any push, pull, and drag techniques ... people will come to you, and it's really awesome doing business that way!

The information I have given you in this chapter is not for the faint of heart—especially not the social media strategy. It's the top 1% kind of stuff.

If you choose to listen to your old mindset, you will likely come up with all kinds of reasons why you can't do this and why it won't work for you ... and as a result, change nothing in your business. If you operate from a *growth mindset,* however, that embraces new challenges and opportunities, you will focus all your energy on being <u>resourceful,</u> you will find the answers you need, do the work, and reap tremendous rewards.

Start demonstrating to people how you are able to help them on their journey from where they *ARE* to where they *WANT* to be, and if you can make this paradigm shift in your marketing … **the rest of this business is a piece of cake.**

To access your FREE book bonuses go to:
www.AlinaSchumacher.com/bookbonuses

SKILL 8

THE BEST OPEN HOUSE STRATEGY TO GET CLIENTS FAST

We have built an incredibly solid foundation. We have prepared the ground, we have planted the right seed, and things are starting to come up. In other words, people are starting to notice you, whether that's on social, or when you're out and about, previewing homes—your brand is starting to gain some great momentum.

Let's keep it going.

If you already have some listings, you're going to love this next strategy because it will help you to maximize your efforts immensely!

If you don't have any listings yet—you're going to love this even more because this will help you to break into the market and get some—*IF* ... and only if you have completed *Stages 1 and 2*.

My coaching Students know this strategy as the "Million Dollar Question" strategy ... and is it ever effective. You're about to find out why.

THE MILLION DOLLAR QUESTION

Open Houses are a real GOLD mine when it comes to **getting clients FAST**—if done strategically. If you don't have any listings to hold open right now, ask someone in your brokerage.

In fact, if you *have* previewed all the inventory in your marketplace and completed all the other preparation steps as I outlined for you in Chapter Five, including the Agent Lunch'n Learn, I don't think you'll have a problem finding an agent who will give you an opportunity.

Ideally, you'll hopefully be able to connect with one of the agents you interviewed. And since you already demonstrated a high level of drive and excellence when you previewed their listings, and courteously gave them feedback on the day after, bought them lunch, and asked them some really great questions that made them pause and think ... *and* sent them a hand-written thank you note ... they are already very aware of you and what you stand for.

Of course, it would be amazing if you could hold an Open House in the area you want to establish in. But even if it's not the perfect location, look at it as a continuation of your boot camp and sharpening your skills.

I have always loved doing Open Houses! For one, **it allowed me to keep my finger on the pulse of the local market**—which is buyers. And buyers not only give you a ton of insight, they are hands down the best source of future listing leads.

Sometimes, I'd even have people visit my open houses with no intention of actually looking at the house. They had heard the buzz, and as I would find out later, just wanted to come by and see how I was handling things because they were thinking of listing their home in the near future.

Those were likely the High-C personality styles, who like to do their research in advance and be prepared. And if they see you organizing people's shoes in the entry, and perhaps even picking up a broom to quickly spot-clean if needed, while engaging your visitors and answering their questions in a knowledgeable and insightful way, you're going to make an impression—but I digressed.

What is the main goal when you're meeting new people at an Open House? Traditionally, most agents' goal is to get *an email address* so they can *add them to their fancy CRM database* (and send automated email newsletters that nobody reads) … right? You and I are going to do this differently. Not like you're surprised or anything.

LET'S PRETEND YOU'RE A PROSPECTIVE BUYER, LOOKING AT OPEN HOUSES

It's a Sunday afternoon and you're looking to get an idea on what's for sale in the area. You've already toured four properties this afternoon and are about to look at property number five. The previous four agents, although all quite nice, had more or less the same process, and by now, you know the drill ... if you know what I mean.

As you enter the home, the agent welcomes you with a big smile, and with a twinkle in her eye, she says, *"Would you prefer to remove your footwear, or would you like to try these really cool new slip-ons I have here to put over your shoes ... the price is a whopping zero dollars!"*

You chuckle, and as you grab a pair of the slip-ons, the agent hands you a really nice, thick sheet of paper. *"Here's a feature sheet for you, and if you don't mind me grabbing your name and phone number really quick? It's just to make sure we know who's been through the home! Sometimes people forget their glasses on the countertop, drop their phone, or kids lose a toy or a sock—you know how it goes! It's also requested by the homeowners. I'm not gonna need an email—just your name and a quick phone number, please."*

Sounds reasonable, and as she scribbles down your name and phone number, she says, *"Btw., may I ask who you're working with?"*

Well, since you just started looking and don't have an agent yet, you reply, *"I actually just started to look. I'm not really working with anyone yet."*

"For sure! Take a look around, and if you have any questions whatsoever, I'm here for you!"

Quick Time Out: Did you catch what we just did there?

We totally interrupted the prospect's rhythm and expectation and very quickly and effectively earned a good chunk of her trust. Why?

1. Clearly, there was a process. That instantly communicates professionalism. Best of all, the prospect didn't have to fill out anything themselves.
2. There's humor. Life is way too serious ... let's be fun to be around!
3. We did the opposite of what the prospect expected (ask for their email). In fact, we said we don't need it. What agent will ever say that?
4. No agent? To the average hungry tiger, that means ... POUNCE! And you just said, '*Take a look around...* '??

Yes. This is how you become **irresistibly magnetic** to your ideal prospects—with class, wit, and style. Now, this buyer prospect is going to be even more open and receptive to the next couple of questions. Watch!

So, What Happens Next?

Let the prospect tour the home! There are a few more qualifying questions I'd typically like to weave in to make sure they are a good fit, like understanding their urgency and motivation for example, but the bottom line is, **if my brain and my intuition are on the same page,** and this sounds like someone I'd like to work with, I'll ask them my Million Dollar Question just as they're getting ready to leave. (Probably in utter amazement and disbelief that I *still* haven't tried to 'convert' them!)

Let's set it up. (You're back in the Buyer role … and I'm the agent.)

"So, what do you think? Is there any specific feedback I can pass on to the homeowners?" To which most *normal* people will say, *"It's nice! They did a great job with the kitchen,"* or something superficial like that.

And this is where things can usually get a little awkward, right?

They're ready to leave, but you still want to know what the deal is! You don't want to be *that agent* and be too direct, and yet … ARE THEY GOING TO BE WRITING AN OFFER? If not, why not? What are you supposed to tell the sellers? Right?

Guess how I know all this stuff!!!

So, here's how you do it…

"May I ask one more question?"

And I'm willing to bet **a whole quarter** that their reply is going to be, *"Sure!"* ... and I happen to have that kind of money.

So, you proceed, *"If you had a magic wand and you could change just one thing about this home, what would it be?"*

And then you shut up and don't say another word. Just listen.

Total and complete game-changer, because **if they are actually a legit buyer** who is really interested in buying something in the near future, they are now going to tell you what they really think, and why they won't be putting in an offer—or in other words, what's most important to them in their next home!

Since you have thoroughly done your prep work in *Stages 1 and 2,* you toured every single home in the area, and took notes on each of those additional questions I gave you, this is where things are starting to pay off!

Because now you can pull out your up to date binder with all the insider information, and demonstrate a level of competence and extra market insight that the OTHER four agents could never touch! Because you know everything there is to know about every single house. You even know how it smells!!

"Oh, did you see the new one that just came on the market yesterday? I have a printout here with some extra info. If you like, I can email it to you, or I could arrange a showing for us—either after the Open House today, or perhaps tomorrow sometime?"

And you literally show them your binder, and flip through ALL the current inventory <u>so they can actually SEE your additional notes with all the extra info on each of those properties,</u> including layout, functionality, cleanliness, upgrades, location, pros and cons, value … I can guarantee you they have never seen anything like that before! *(Unless they met a World-Class Agent who's been through my training, of course.)*

The impact and effect of this simple strategy is out of this world, and **if you want to finally stop wasting your Sunday afternoons** and actually start attracting serious and qualified prospects and converting them into not just clients but raving fans, that's how you do it!

NOW LET'S TAKE THIS STRATEGY TO THE NEXT LEVEL AND GET SOME LISTINGS

You've got some great new clients to work with. Now let's demonstrate to them that **you don't just set them up on an auto-search** and wait for the right place to hit the market! Any agent can do that.

You want to be *LISTING* that perfect property yourself because chances are that what they're looking for isn't on the market right now.

PERFECT!

And even if there are a few options on the market that somewhat fit their criteria, **you still want to do this next step.**

It's literally one of **the best and most profitable listing-generating strategies I've ever used**—and it's *Wanted Ads*—but not how you might think.

The local community paper works best for this <u>but NOT the classified section.</u> This is crucial. I always ran ads on the inside cover, or page three of the paper—and always in color.

Quick Time Out: Does anyone even read the paper nowadays? Absolutely. Most communities have a local newspaper that is all about local events and happenings, local sports updates, up and coming football/hockey stars, letters to the editor, zoning issues, citizen complaints, etc. And people with money (and houses) still do read the paper.

So, if anyone tells you that **this strategy is outdated**—great!

More listings for you.

<u>Here's the ad template:</u>

"Urgently Wanted in Springfield! Young family looking for 2-3 bedroom home close to Oakbank, preferably with attached garage. Up to 350K. Call Alina at 444.3000 for more info!"

This strategy is like a CASH machine, because it gets people's curiosity, and it communicates that you are an active agent in the area who's got buyers.

Plus, it gets the people who are thinking of selling sometime in the future to come out of the woodwork and give you a <u>priority opportunity to do a CMA</u> and build a solid relationship with them before anyone else even knows about it.

Here's what it usually sounds like, *"Oh hi, I saw your ad in the paper and we were going to list in a few months, but if these people like what we have, and the price is right, we may be willing to sell sooner."*

PERFECT!

And since you've done your homework and been to every single active listing in town, you will immediately have a fairly good idea on what that place is worth and ... have the data to back it up!

Yes, the magic binder that most agents think is silly and outdated.

Oh, well.

The bottom line is that it's *so much easier* to do business, when people reach out to you, instead of you having to chase them, isn't it? All because you took the time to prepare and completed *Stages 1 and 2* of the Market Domination plan first! Now, it's time to exceed your clients' expectations with a World-Class *Experience* and turn them into lifetime clients and raving fans.

SKILL 9

YOUR SIGNATURE SELLING SYSTEMS AND PROCESSES

We are finally in *Stage 4* of the Market Domination Plan, which is all about creating that world-class signature *Experience* for your clients. Going forward, this is where the bulk of your time will be spent because if you do an outstanding job for your clients and help them get from where they are to where they want to be, and stay in touch in a meaningful way, they will be clients for life, and refer their friends and family. Which means that you don't have to spend all your time, energy, and money on *prospecting* activities like you used to in order to survive.

Instead, you can focus on growing, stabilizing, and systematizing all the moving parts of your business, start building your world-class support team, and ultimately turn your **solo-preneur job into an actual business** that continues to cashflow without you having to work every evening and weekend!

That's the Ultimate Goal.

Now, before you start daydreaming about where you want to retire, come back to me for a second ... we still have a little more work to do!

Although, it *is* pretty awesome to be able to travel multiple times a year, knowing that your business will continue to run like a well-oiled machine even without you. And the time for that will come.

Right now, let's start thinking about what you want that world-class client *Experience* to look like, and then create the systems and processes that will help you to execute that experience as efficiently and consistently as possible.

To do that, <u>let's start with the end in mind.</u> Picture your ideal client with a SOLD sign in their yard. You just sold their property and also helped them find their new family dream home. They are beyond ecstatic with the results and the *Experience* they had working with you!

Tell me, what exactly would had to have happened for them to think and feel that way? And what specific aspects of that experience would be so unique and remarkable (in the truest sense of the word) that they wouldn't hesitate to tell their friends and family about it?

Remember the opening story in the very first chapter of this book, where I shared about my experience at the Gustino restaurant?

If you think about … **it didn't really take *THAT* much extra** to make the experience remarkable and memorable, did it?

1. The staff greeted us by our names as we walked in.
2. They were extremely well trained, attentive, and helpful.
3. The food and the ambiance were fantastic.
4. There was a live saxophone player.
5. And finally ... the red rose.

Would It Be Hard or Expensive to Replicate this Experience at ANY Restaurant, Anywhere in the World?

Not at all!

Could any restaurant owner travel to some of the finest dining places in the world, get some great ideas, design their own signature experience, train their staff, and create a work environment where the staff are actually motivated to exceed expectations, and with that, get people to come back, and bring their friends and family? No doubt.

Will every restaurant do that?

IT'S YOUR TURN

It doesn't take very much to get your clients' attention, and surprise them with something special and thoughtful that will still be remembered for many years to come.

Something as simple as a hand-written thank you note that gets mailed right after the property is listed, a generous bouquet of fresh flowers for the Open House, and a beautiful dinner together, as soon as the property is sold are relatively inexpensive ways to nurture a long-term client relationship and express gratitude.

The most important thing is consistency, because if one client has a really great experience, and everything is extremely well choreographed and executed, but then another client doesn't get that same world-class treatment … because it's a busier season and you're not able to keep up, word will spread. People talk either way.

What do you want them to say?

An intentionally created *Experience* and a relentless <u>consistency</u> in executing and upholding the standards of that experience is one of the greatest and most important components of a successful brand, and you achieve that by creating <u>measurable and duplicable</u> systems and processes.

Intentionally Designed Systems & Processes Will Help You To:

- Provide <u>all</u> your clients with the same, consistent, world-class experience
- Stop losing prospects and repeat clients because you forgot to *[insert blank]*

- Create loyal, life-time clients who refer their friends and family
- Get more things done *FASTER*
- Save a lot of time, energy, frustration, and resources
- Evaluate, measure, improve, and scale your business, etc.

Quick Timeout: *What's the Difference Between a System and a Process?*

Anything you do repeatedly is essentially a system. Let's take brushing your teeth, for example. Since you do it every day, it's your system for keeping your teeth clean and healthy. The process would consist of each chronological step you'd have to take to execute that system. In other words, every morning you go to the bathroom sink, you take your toothbrush, you make it wet, you put some toothpaste on it, you brush your teeth … red to white, etc.

You could go really ninja, and tape a checklist to your bathroom mirror to make sure you didn't forget a step! But that, in a nutshell, is the definition, and the difference.

I cannot tell you how many agents I have worked with over the past few years who have all consistently told me that **their greatest struggle in business is a LACK of SYSTEMS.**

"I just need to get some systems in place!"

Personally, even though my *I* is quite high on the DISC, my *C* is also very high, and so ... please don't hate me ... but I've always been a list maker. Even with things as simple as having company over for dinner, you will find a list on my kitchen countertop that outlines what I am going to make, plus a timeline of when each item goes in the oven, or needs to be prepped, warmed up, etc., to make sure everything gets done properly and at the right time.

On the Enneagram, I'm a Two *(Helper/Befriender)* with a very strong One *wing (Improver/Perfectionist)*. In other words, I would rather die than not help you get organized, especially if you ask for it!

And, so, after listening to my coaching clients for a while, telling me about this 'system problem', and coaching them through the process multiple times, giving them all my best tips, they would still come back with the same problem. It puzzled me!

And then it dawned on me ...

Their problem wasn't a lack of systems, per se. <u>Everybody has systems and a certain way of doing things.</u> It might not be the most efficient and effective one, but it's a system, nonetheless.

When agents are complaining about needing *better* systems, what they're *REALLY* saying is that they don't have clearly outlined and easy to follow processes in place **to execute those systems.**

In other words, to use the tooth brushing analogy, they generally know what they have to do when it comes to keeping their teeth clean. But one day, they brush and floss, the next day, they brush and forget to floss, the day after they're out of toothpaste, so they brush without it. You get the point.

The simplest solution would be to write out every single step they need to take chronologically—which is the process—and then create a checklist with those steps, and tape it to their bathroom mirror. And then follow that checklist every single day until it becomes second nature and runs on auto-pilot.

Your Real Estate Business Is No Different

To create the kind of systems and processes that will enable you to manage your daily activities in the most efficient way, let's write down every action step you're already doing now, and then let's see how we can organize and bring a consistent structure to everything, improve what's lacking, add what's missing, and simplify what's confusing.

To get started …

Let's Organize Your Current Activities Into the Following Categories:

<u>**Buyers**</u>

- The exact action steps you take to qualify a prospect and convert them into a buyer
- The exact action steps you take to help them find a home
- The exact action steps you take once their offer has been accepted
- The exact action steps you take once the buyer has moved into the new house

<u>**Sellers**</u>

- The exact action steps you take to do a property evaluation
- The exact action steps you take immediately after the listing is signed
- The exact action steps you take once an offer has been accepted
- The exact action steps you take after the property is sold

…and everything in-between.

For example, let's take Step One in working with Buyers. Here are the type of questions I would ask you if I coached you through this process to help you flesh that out:

1. When you meet a new prospect, what is your typical process to qualify them?

2. Do you do that via email, phone, or in person?

3. Do you require a face-to-face meeting to form the agency relationship?

4. What kind of questions do you ask to make sure they are financially qualified?

5. Do you require any type of documentation as proof?

6. How do you determine their level of motivation and urgency?

7. What questions do you ask to understand what they're looking for?

8. Do you take copies of their IDs?

9. Do you mail them a hand-written thank you note or send it via email?

10. How do you communicate with them and how often?

11. How do they get notified about new listings?

12. Do you require them to do a drive-by before you schedule an official showing?

You get the point.

Ideally, try to block off 4-5 hours of uninterrupted time to get this done. If you're like most normal human beings, you'd rather be out and about, working with people than writing out lists and processes. I get that.

Let's do it anyway, and I promise, your feelings are going to catch up when people start asking how in the world you're able to get so much done.

Once you've completed this *brain dump,* so to speak, and you have chronologically organized everything you do into the categories I just outlined, let's take a look at what could be simplified or streamlined, as well as added or improved. What parts can be outsourced? What action steps need to get scheduled in your phone so you never ever forget to do them?

Remember, the **purpose of systems and processes** is <u>to make life easier</u>—not more complicated.

We had a system and process for everything, even how we installed and maintained our signage, and how long our signs stayed up *after* a property was sold!

Because, instead of becoming a landmark in town, I wanted to create the impression that my For-Sale signs were never around for too long, which, when you think about, is the exact opposite of what most agents are doing, isn't it?

Most agents' strategy is to leave that SOLD sign up for as long as possible to get as much exposure as possible. But if you think about it ... once you've seen it, you've seen it. And if you're driving past that sign every single day, pretty soon you stop paying attention and don't even notice it anymore.

When my properties sold and my husband installed the **FINISHED** signs—main and all directionals—he would immediately schedule a pick up reminder on his phone for exactly two weeks later.

Because even those seemingly small things can make a big difference in how people perceive your brand and value in the marketplace.

Now, before you think that I am Superwoman—which I'm not—let me tell you ... it didn't start that way.

It's one thing to love lists and being able to manage yourself, it's an entirely different thing to lead a team, and train and empower them to help you manage a business.

Eventually, I got so busy, though, I simply had to figure out an actual system and detailed process for everything because otherwise it either meant **looking stupid in front of my clients** because I (or one of my team members) had dropped the ball on something ... again, or it meant coming home exhausted, remembering the things I had forgotten to do, **and then having to play catch-up all night when all I wanted to do was spend time with my family.**

To Summarize:

Having systems and a step-by-step process on how you execute those systems will enable you to provide your clients with a consistent world-class *Experience* and fuel your future repeat and referral business. And if you now **add some detailed checklists** to keep track of you and your team's activities and utilize the power of technology for reminders—oh, Happy Day!

THE POWER OF CHECKLISTS

The other day, as I was going through a shoebox filled with some of my most cherished memorabilia, I came across a checklist that I had written back in February of 1995, planning my husband's and my engagement party with our church youth group. I had to chuckle about it.

It's interesting how simple and clear things become once you write them on a piece of paper, and how much easier it is to get things done, when you're following a simple checklist.

Checklists are awesome, and we had one for pretty much everything at the office. You may need to customize this based on your market area, of course, but **here are a few ideas on what we used:**

- CMA checklists that helped me to remember all the data I needed to collect in order to arrive at the most accurate property value
- Buyer profile checklists
- Electronic filing checklists
- Property showing and feedback checklists
- Deal processing checklists
- Etc.

In fact, **when my brokerage was <u>audited by the Securities Commission</u>** the very first year we were in business, which unbeknownst to me was standard procedure for new brokerages, the Registrar remarked on the fact that he had never seen paperwork in such well-organized manner, and especially appreciated the deal processing checklists that we had stapled to the inside cover of every file. That was pretty cool for a rookie broker!

And when you're ready to expand, checklists also make it super easy to onboard new team members, and monitor, course-correct, and praise their performance! In fact, let's talk about **my best hiring and team-building strategies,** and the important shift you absolutely must make—at the right time—in order to start dominating your market FAST.

Because let's face it, <u>it's hard to dominate and have a life,</u> if you're a one-man show, right?

YOUR WORLD-CLASS SUPPORT TEAM

Let me quickly acknowledge you. Most people typically don't make it past the introduction ... and you're already building a team! Pretty awesome stuff!

All your hard work is finally starting to pay off, you're building more and more momentum **and starting to make some money,** <u>and now you have a very important decision to make.</u> Either you keep hustling and keep doing everything yourself because you're worried that this isn't going to last, and you don't want the responsibility of having someone on your payroll if the market slows down. Plus ... to be completely honest, you don't really want to part with that extra 30K a year.

Or you make this next, important shift, and you make it at the right time, you step out of your *new* comfort zone, and make that very first hire. Specifically, a really good <u>un</u>licensed assistant who is going to *manage* all of those systems and processes for you, and make everything run like that well-oiled machine we were talking about earlier.

After all, you don't make money doing admin work—you make money selling houses. And your hour is worth a lot more than the

$15+ dollars you're going to be paying someone else to do that admin work for you.

Ideally, you'll want to find someone who is a *High S* with a good amount of *High C*. This personality style is kind, friendly, attentive to details, and really good with people!

They absolutely flourish in a support role where it's all about helping others. Just make sure to provide a steady and balanced work environment as well as clearly outlined, step-by-step instructions. Without that, they will get more and more frustrated, because, if you remember from Chapter Two, uncertainty is one of their greatest fears.

They do, however, love checklists and they love to finish things, knowing that they have done it well and according to expectations. If you create that type of work environment for them, they will become your right hand, and they will be forever loyal to you.

The wrong personality style (for this particular position) would be someone who is a *High D* or a *High I*—both a catastrophe— because the *High D* hates details and doesn't have a lot of patience for this sort of work, and the *High I* will be spending way too much time socializing and forget half the things you asked them to do.

Both of these styles love freedom, creativity, risk, and being in control, and if you make the mistake of hiring someone like that, because "they're just like you and you instantly hit it off,"—I hate to disappoint you, but they won't be there for very long.

Ask me how I know…

I've trained more than just one of my <u>direct competitors,</u> because **apparently, I'm a slow learner.**

You see, these personality styles are going to be doing the work for a while, and once they've learned everything there is to know, and the excitement and the thrill is gone, they are going to get bored … and have an epiphany … *"Man, this is actually not that hard! I'm just gonna get my license and start selling real estate myself!"* (And they will actually be really good at it.)

HOW TO FIND THE RIGHT PEOPLE

So, how do you find the right people, and how do you know what their personality style is? Easy! Just ask them to take the test *BEFORE* the actual interview! In other words, once you collect all the resumes, if that's the route you go, send them a link to an online test, and kindly ask them to send you a copy of the full report as step one of the qualifying process.

If you choose to pursue a referral by a trusted source, I would still recommend to not skip this step.

Then, after you determine that the personality style looks like a good fit, invite the candidate for a personal interview. If that goes well, <u>don't make the common mistake to stop at this stage.</u>

In my hiring process, there are two more crucial steps.

Step one: I would invite the potential candidate AND their spouse or significant other to a dinner with myself and my husband. And this may sound unusual, but this strategy not only enables you to observe how your potential new employee treats you and your spouse in a more relaxed atmosphere, but also shows how they treat their partner as well as the servers or staff.

You'd be surprised how much this can reveal about the true character and values of the person you're considering to hire.

And since that person is going to be representing you and the very first impression people are going to have of you when they call your office - this matters a lot!

Step two: Let's invite the finalist to a full trial day at work. This step is crucial. And granted, there will be nerves, and since your systems and processes are probably not quite ironed out yet, this step isn't so much about the actual *work*, per se.

It's about you being able to assess their listening and comprehension skills, computer skills, typing and spelling skills, their communication skills, and … their critical thinking skills. While you'll want to make sure that you are extra gracious, understanding, and patient with your candidate, this strategy enables you to observe how they handle their own blunders or mistakes—whether those are due to miscommunication or lack of current knowledge and skill.

Frankly, I will take someone <u>who isn't quite as qualified</u> in terms of their skillset, but has a great attitude, a teachable and humble spirit, and is able to acknowledge a mistake and take responsibility for it, over someone who has all the skills AND an arrogant, know-it-all kind of attitude—any time.

Because I can teach skill. It's hard to teach attitude and responsibility.

Once you've completed this final step in your hiring process and you've chosen the right candidate, **make sure to present them with a proper contract.** You and I are probably okay with a handshake, but their personality style is all about stability and safety, remember?

A contract that clearly spells out your expectations is very important to them, and it should include any and all details on annual salary, potential benefits, vacation, probation period, evaluation dates, as well as a termination policy. If you'd like to get a sample of the contracts I used, you'll find that at www.alinaschumacher. com/bookbonuses

ONE FINAL WORD ON TIMING

The decision to make that very first hire is important because doing everything yourself is not only impossible to scale, **it'll eventually burn you out.** However, *when* to make that decision is of equal importance, because many agents make it too late.

The reason is simple.

They realize that they're getting busier and busier and that they really need to get some help. But because they don't know <u>how</u> to find the right person, **they procrastinate.** Besides, there is also this notion that, *"No one can do it like me, and definitely not as fast!"*

Eventually, though, the bucket is full. They keep dropping the ball and forgetting things, they are frustrated, clients aren't as happy as they used to be, and the side effect is that <u>they're starting to kill their own momentum.</u>

And because of all that pressure, there is no time for an intentionally thought out hiring process, so they hire the first person that seems qualified. And since they don't have the time or systems in place to properly train them, their frustration level escalates and leaves a bitter taste in everyone's mouth.

Don't let it come to that.

Instead of Hiring *Fast* and Firing *Slow* ... Hire *SLOW* and Fire *FAST!*

While I believe in providing people with the proper work environment and giving them ample time to learn and grow into their new position, if you know in your heart of hearts that you made a mistake and hired the wrong person, **don't make the bigger mistake of hanging on to them** ... hoping that they'll eventually come around.

If they haven't gotten it until now, they probably never will. That doesn't make them a bad person, just not the right one for your world-class support team. <u>Set them free</u> and allow them the opportunity to find the type of work and work environment that they'll enjoy more.

There are so many great, and very talented people out there that actually care! Just take the time to follow the exact steps I outlined in this chapter, and I promise, you will find the perfect team member who really will make your business run flawlessly.

One last skill that is going to tie it all together and liberate you to **structure your business so that it serves you, instead of you being enslaved to it,** and missing out on the most important things in life ...

SKILL 10

THE WISDOM TO SAY NO

One of the hardest things for me to do in life and in business is saying *NO* to people. I mean, I am a recovering people-pleaser, and I would rather overcommit and overextend myself than disappoint anyone.

Have you ever felt that way? Have you ever said, "*YES!*" to something, when everything on the inside of you was screaming "*NO!*"?

I think **it takes a really special kind of person to be a real estate agent.** On one hand, there is this huge opportunity to help people and make a really great income doing so. On the other hand, however, there is a tremendous amount of risk and uncertainty that you have to be willing to take because you're essentially committing to doing all the work upfront, you have to spend your own money and resources to get the job done—and yet, there is *NO* guarantee that you're actually going to get paid!

After all, you can't guarantee that the house is going to sell, right?

Therefore, I believe that to truly succeed at this business long-term, you must not only be willing to embrace that risk while being extremely confident in your ability to get the job done, you must have a very sharp sense and ability to balance between your desire to help people because you care … <u>and knowing when to walk away.</u>

Personally, I had to learn that lesson the hard way, and I would say yes to pretty much everything, no matter how impossible the circumstances or how glaring the **warning signs**.

And I'm not just talking about taking on overpriced listings at discount commissions or listing vacant homes, promising to *"look after everything and taking care of the yard until it sells"* … although, clearly, I am talking from experience.

But if you've ever worked with abusive, hard-core divorce cases, suicidal alcoholics, and serious drug addicts, you know what I'm talking about, because it is impossible to just turn off your thoughts when you come home to your family.

I was determined to help everyone, regardless of how difficult the situation. After all, I am not a quitter, and I don't give up, right? Eventually … I crashed and burned out.

This business is incredibly demanding, and if you're not careful, it can take over your entire life. You won't ever be able to help everyone, no matter how hard you try and how deeply you care. And the truth is, not everyone wants to be helped.

Sometimes we want more for people than they want for themselves. And some people will be demanding, complicated and pretty much impossible to please no matter what you do.

Obviously, I am not saying that you should walk away from anything that poses a potential challenge.

Just <u>be aware of your boundaries and professional duties and responsibilities</u> and never forget that **saying *YES* to something usually means saying *NO* to something else.** How many times in life do we accept what we should be rejecting … and put on the back burner what should really be a priority?

Let's take a few moments to reflect and do some deep soul-searching.

If today was your last day to live, what would be your greatest regret in life?

I realize this is a very heavy question, but are you brave enough to answer it? If today really was your very last day to live, what do you wish you would have done … or done more of? Who would you have taken more time for, perhaps called, reconciled with … or forgiven?

Ponder these questions for a few minutes, and when you're ready, grab a piece of paper and write down the things that are most important to you in life—the things (and the people) that you couldn't and wouldn't want to live without.

Here's the moment of truth:

If those things (and people) really are most important to you in life … *when are you going to start treating them that way?*

What is in the way?

- Perhaps you feel guilty about not spending enough quality time (yes quality, present-in-the-moment, without your phone kind of time) with your family.
- Maybe you've stopped believing in your own New Year's resolutions because you've broken more commitments to yourself than you can count, and you've been failing to achieve your goals year after year because something or someone else usually takes priority over doing something for yourself.
- You've been wanting to eat cleaner and healthier, finally start a regular workout routine, take more time off, go on that special vacation with your family, or start reading more books—if only there was more time in a day!

If you *DON'T* want to wake up one day … and it actually being your last one, and those regrets having slowly become your reality, it's time to make a change. After all, if nothing changes, nothing changes.

WHAT ARE YOUR *TRUE* PRIORITIES IN LIFE?

Steven Covey calls this the Big Rock principle. If you picture a jar, a bunch of large rocks, smaller rocks, some gravel, and some sand—these would be the big rocks, representing the most important things in your life. The non-negotiables, so to speak. However, unless you actually put them into the jar *first*, they won't fit in.

Sadly, that is how most people live their entire lives. They're sorting sand and gravel all day long, and at the end of the day, when the jar is almost full, they try to fit in those big rocks, but they just won't fit in.

How often have you said *YES* to a last-minute appointment, or a drive-by prospect who "absolutely has to see the house in the next 15 minutes", which means you have to cancel or reschedule something you had already planned with your family?

Maybe it's just me, and you've never struggled with this kind of stuff?

When I first heard about the principle of time-blocking from my mentor, Michael Hyatt, it literally changed my life. In fact, when I started to apply the technique and became relentless and systematic about putting first things first, being more rigorous in prequalifying my prospects, and **booking appointments on *my* terms**—I finally got my life back! (And most of my weekends.)

And that's what I want for you because I know it's possible.

See, every time someone requests you to do something for them, and that particular time slot **isn't officially blocked off in your calendar**, you'll probably almost always give in and say *"YES"* ... even though you may have already had plans for that particular time.

You may have wanted to do something with your family, go to the gym, attend your daughter's piano recital, or it might have been that Wednesday night baseball practice with your little guy. *REGARDLESS,* you meant well, and at that particular time, your mind didn't even register the conflict.

You genuinely forgot!

But when you come home in the evening, you have to once again explain to your little one, why Mommy or Daddy had to go and show houses again tonight ... that is ... if they aren't in bed already because they fell asleep waiting for you.

THERE IS A MUCH BETTER WAY

What if you actually did consider the things that you do on a daily basis as rocks of different sizes based on their level of priority? And what if you took that imaginary jar, which represents your daily schedule, and you started by putting in those big rocks that are absolutely non-negotiable *first*, and *then* added the smaller rocks, and eventually the gravel, and the sand? Do you think the smaller rocks and all that sand and gravel would still fit in-between those big rocks? You bet.

What are Those Big Rocks for You?

What deserves top priority when you zoom out and look at the bigger picture of your life? Here are some of the things that I schedule (or used to schedule) before anything else:

- My morning routine.
- Dates with my husband.
- Individual dates with my kids on the day of their birthday each month. We started doing this back in the summer of 2012, and I cannot even begin to tell you how many amazing conversations we've had over dessert, breakfast or lunch, a round of golf, or just a walk at the park. Priceless.
- Our family vacations.
- House cleaning and laundry. I have a professional helping me with that on a weekly basis because my time is worth so

much more than what I'm paying them to do that for me. Plus, I know it'll get done. Find a reliable and trustworthy cleaner using the hiring strategies I taught in the previous chapter. You want someone who is task and detail-oriented. And even though, the dinner with the spouse might be overkill, definitely do a trial day. Hide a few coins—yes, I'm serious—and the person that finds all the change … and hands it in … is a keeper!

- At least two weekends per month off.
- My Saturdays. Here's why: Since I'd often do Open Houses on Sunday afternoons, I made sure that my Saturdays were <u>always</u> off. I firmly believe that we all need a day of dedicated rest per week. Look, even God rested on the seventh day of creation to get refreshed—which simply means to breathe *in*—and we should, too. It's important to unplug and recharge on a regular basis.
- Personal growth, conferences, training, coaching, etc.
- Family nights—games, movie, pizza … and no phones!

Schedule *EVERYTHING* into your calendar and treat it like official appointments. For real.

If you had the opportunity to meet <u>your absolute favorite artist, athlete, or actor</u>—someone you totally admire and respect, would you cancel that appointment last minute, just because someone just drove by one of your listings and wanted to see it in an hour?

I think not. It's called priorities.

And now, whenever someone calls and requests your service, you can look at your calendar, and if you already have a commitment at that particular time—and the request is not time-sensitive—you can elegantly and unapologetically say, *"Oh, I wish I could, but ... I already have a commitment at that time. How about Thursday at 4 pm instead, or would 6 pm work better for you?"*

See how easy that is?

I can promise you, a serious prospect/client will never expect you to jump within the hour. In fact, I believe they'll respect you even more if you address them the way I just suggested.

AND **... you'll finally get to watch that baseball practice!**

Remember, saying *YES* to something usually means saying *NO* to something else. To build and sustain a truly successful and lasting real estate business that ultimately supports the quality lifestyle you desire, you must know when, who, and what to say *NO* to and have the courage and freedom to walk away without it stealing your peace and joy. Only then will you be liberated to direct your undivided focus to the things and the people that deserve your *YES!*

FINAL THOUGHTS

The real estate business truly is one of the best businesses to be in. It has afforded my family and me a lifestyle I could have never dreamed of. We are truly blessed, not only to be able to enjoy the fruit of our labor, but even more importantly ... to share it with others.

And it is my great wish for you to apply the principles and strategies I've shared in this book, become the most knowledgeable, competent, and trusted agent in your marketplace, serve with utmost excellence and dedication, and live the life of your dreams!

To access your FREE book bonuses go to:
www.AlinaSchumacher.com/bookbonuses

Made in the USA
Middletown, DE
13 March 2021